PRAISE FOR *PASS IT ON*

"What great memories! Mary Kay was influential in Dad's career, allowing him to pre-sell his first book, *See You at the Top*, when he spoke at her events in order to help fund its publication before it was even printed. He had great respect and gratitude toward this amazingly genuine friend, and *Pass it On* is a tremendous tribute to a very special woman."

—TOM ZIGLAR, CEO of Ziglar, Inc. and proud son of Zig Ziglar

"This book is an inspiration to everyone who is blessed to read it! It's filled with wisdom, timeless principles, and true stories of how Mary Kay Ash deeply impacted the lives of countless thousands by living out her faith testimony in life and in business! The legacy she passed on to me also has been passed on to my daughters and granddaughters. She was a generation changer!"

—KATHY HELOU, Inner Circle National Sales Director
and Emerald National Sales Director

"Mary Kay Ash was my dear friend. Kudos to Jennifer Cook for penning a book that is filled with wonderful stories and reveals the warmth and wisdom of one of America's great entrepreneurs."

—ROBERT L. SHOOK, *New York Times*, Best-selling Author

D1496345

"'God has purpose for us,' says the apostle Paul in Romans 5:3–4. In Jennifer Cook's *Pass it on*, she recounts Mary Kay Ash's story. Jennifer describes Mary Kay's start from meager means, her effect on the lives of thousands of people through her global billion-dollar business, and the dramatic effect she had on Jennifer's life. God used her trials and blessings to mold Mary Kay's transformative faith for purposes of sharing the gift of eternity with others through her business, just as God had purpose in Jennifer sharing her story."

—DIANE PADDISON, Founder and President of 4word,
and Author of *Work, Love, Pray and Be Refreshed . . .*
A year of devotions for women in the workplace

"I met Jennifer Cook after Mary Kay was no longer on this earth, and she has faithfully shared Mary Kay's example of love and caring, making Mary Kay real. I know this book will help many other women to find success in all areas of their lives, and they, in turn, will be inspired to Pass It On."

—BIRGIT JOHNSON, National Sales Director, Germany

Many people have asked how it was that Mary Kay Ash was able to lead women in a manner that was uncommon to how the world operated. Leadership in our company was grounded in love and in the power of Belief. She believed in us, so we were able to believe in ourselves. Women thrive and flourish in that kind of atmosphere and Mary Kay understood that truth. Jennifer Cook has brilliantly and beautifully shown us who Mary Kay the Christian was, and how that changed lives.

— STACY JAMES, Inner Circle National Sales Director

PASS
IT ON

PASS IT ON

What I Learned from MARY KAY ASH

JENNIFER BICKEL COOK

BROWN BOOKS
PUBLISHING GROUP

Pass it On
What I Learned from Mary Kay Ash

Brown Books Publishing Group
Dallas, TX / New York, NY
www.BrownBooks.com
(972) 381-0009

A New Era in Publishing®

Publisher's Cataloging-In-Publication Data

Names: Cook, Jennifer Bickel, author.
Title: Pass it on : what I learned from Mary Kay Ash / Jennifer Bickel Cook.
Description: Dallas, TX ; New York, NY : Brown Books Publishing Group, [2021]
Identifiers: ISBN 9781612545233 (paperback)
Subjects: LCSH: Ash, Mary Kay--Influence. | Cook, Jennifer Bickel. | Businesswomen--United States--Biography. | LCGFT: Biographies. | Autobiographies.
Classification: LCC HD9970.5.C672 C66 2021 | DDC 381/.456685/0922 B--dc23

ISBN 978-1-61254-523-3
LCCN 2021908346

Printed in the United States
10 9 8 7 6 5 4 3 2 1

For more information or to contact the author, please go to www.BookPassItOn.com.

To my mentor, Mary Kay Ash,
and my parents, George and Mary Bickel,
the great influencers in my life.

TABLE OF CONTENTS

PREFACE

As a new Christian, I loved the words to Kurt Kaiser's hymn, *Pass It On,* so I remember well the day Mary Kay Ash came into the Mary Kay Inc. corporate headquarters, excited after hearing it for the first time. She said to me, "It expresses so beautifully what I have been saying for years."

> It only takes a spark to get a fire going,
> And soon all those around, can warm up in its glowing.
> That's how it is with God's love once you've experienced it;
> you spread His love to everyone;
> You want to pass it on.[1]

Mary Kay shared her love of God with those around her. She also encouraged others to share the things for which they were grateful. Many times, when women would ask Mary Kay what they could do to thank her for her influence in their lives, I would hear her say, "Pass it on."

That's why I'm writing this book—not only to pass on the stories and lessons I learned from Mary Kay, but to share how they impacted my Christian walk both at work and with my family. Just as Mary Kay conveyed the love of God to me and to others, my hope is to share her faith, wisdom, and wit with you.

Having worked directly with Mary Kay Ash for twenty-five years and observing firsthand how she reacted in various situations, I heard her thoughts and memories on many subjects. After she passed away, I began speaking to the Mary Kay independent sales force and other groups about Mary Kay. So many of these women loved the anecdotes

I related about Mary Kay that they encouraged me to write a book about her.

After retiring from Mary Kay Inc. in 2017, I thought a lot about Mary Kay Ash and her legacy.[2] First and foremost, she would want to be remembered as a servant of Christ. She thought it important to be known as a follower of Jesus, and she lived her life as a testimony to Him.

I finally decided her testimony and example as a Christian businesswoman had to be told. This book contains my personal memories of Mary Kay and recollections from others who knew her well. These stories depict Mary Kay as an entrepreneur, role model, boss, and—most importantly—a woman of faith. No matter which role she played, she was always a Christian first. I have heard many testimonies from sales force members and others whom she inspired to renew their faith or to consider Christianity for the first time.

Mary Kay inspired loyalty. Many of the stories in this book come from a core group who worked closely with Mary Kay for decades: Erma Thomson, Mary Kay's personal assistant; Becky Brown, who served on Mary Kay's secretarial team; and Nancy Thomason, Supervisor of Special Services and Executive Protection Specialist for Mary Kay. After Mary Kay's death, Becky, Nancy, and I worked together on the Mary Kay Museum and The Mary Kay Foundation staff. We believed in Mary Kay's vision and legacy and worked tirelessly to keep her principles alive once she no longer led the company. This book is a memoir, not an autobiography or a biography of Mary Kay Ash. It is largely based on the time I spent with Mary Kay Ash from 1971 until 1995. I heard her speak at many events over this period where she told her personal story, and—after transcribing many of her speeches—much of what she said I know by heart or can at least paraphrase. Fortunately, as there were other witnesses to many of these events, this book or parts of this book have been shared with other staff and independent sales force members who knew her well to ensure as accurate an account as possible.

That being said, memories are a perspective, and others may remember the same incidents with different details. As author Lorrie Moore wrote, "Things, I know, stiffen and shift in memory, become what they never were before."[3] *Pass It On* is written from my head, but also from my heart. It is a labor of love and a personal tribute to an extraordinary woman who founded a multi-billion-dollar corporation, yet remained humble on her journey to success and fame.

ACKNOWLEDGMENTS

As Mary Kay so succinctly said, "Most successful people will tell you: 'If it were not for the help of other people, I wouldn't be where I am today.' I believe that everybody who accomplishes something great has had help from someone. Somebody, somewhere, provided a spark of inspiration, offered a challenge, or held out a hand along the way."

This book could not have been written without the input and encouragement of many people. First of all, my longtime coworkers Erma Thomson, Nancy Thomason, Becky Brown, and Marcelle Trammell not only encouraged me but also helped confirm details in many of the stories. I am especially grateful to the National Sales Directors and National Sales Directors Emeritus who shared their memories of Mary Kay with me.

Thank you to Harry Warren of *The 700 Club* for sending me videos of Mary Kay's appearances. The librarians at the Irving Public Library were not only enthusiastic about this project but also helpful with research questions I had. With much gratitude I want to acknowledge Barry McCoy of McCoy's Classic Portraits, who photographed Mary Kay for many years and has allowed me to use some of his work.

Other friends and family who read chapters, made suggestions, let me bounce ideas off them, and, most importantly, lent their moral support include Stacy Graves, Carol Jo Smith, Diane Paddison, and my daughter Mary Elizabeth Pugh. You gave me confidence to pursue and continue this project.

I also want to thank those at Brown Books Publishing Group who saw the merit in this book and added their expertise to its fulfillment. Being an avid reader, I know that a good book always has a good editor, and I had a great one in Nan Bauroth.

Writing a book consumes many hours. I appreciate my husband Rodney for his patience. I can't count the times I told him, "I can't right now. I am working on my book." My daughter, Mary Elizabeth, and my sons, Christopher and Stephen, have always believed in me and believed in this book. I love you all.

MARY KAY TIMELINE

1918   Mary Kathlyn Wagner is born.

1939   Mary Kay joins Stanley Home Products.

1952   Mary Kay joins World Gift.

1963   Mary Kay launches Beauty by Mary Kay.

1964   Mary Kay holds the first Mary Kay Seminar.

1968   Mary Kay Inc. goes public with over-the-counter stock.

1969   Mary Kay Inc. introduces the Pink Cadillac program.

1971   Mary Kay Inc. opens its first global subsidiary.

1976   Mary Kay stock is listed on the New York Stock Exchange.

1979   Mary Kay is featured in a *60 Minutes* television segment.

1985   Mary Kay Inc. goes private in a leveraged buyout (LBO).

1993   The Mary Kay Museum opens in Dallas, Texas.

1996   Mary Kay suffers a debilitating stroke.

1996   The Mary Kay Foundation is established.

2001   Mary Kay passes away.

2003   Mary Kay is honored as the Greatest Female Entrepreneur in American History by Baylor University.

2020   Mary Kay is named one of the 100 Women of the Century by *USA Today*.

1

MARY KAY'S STORY

She perceives that her merchandise is profitable.
Her lamp does not go out at night.

PROVERBS 31:18

Prior to starting Mary Kay Cosmetics . . . I was a single
working mother supporting three children . . . I know what it's
like to spend an entire day working, away from my family, and
then come home late at night without a single order . . . I try
never to forget these experiences. I want to be able to recall
them so I can relate to another person's problems when she
comes to me for guidance—or a shoulder to cry on.

MARY KAY ASH[1]

Mary Kathlyn Wagner was born May 12, 1918, in Hot Wells, Texas. You won't find Hot Wells on a map today, because the town burned to the ground. When Mary Kay was young, her family moved to the Sixth Ward in Houston, Texas. Mary Kay's siblings were much older and had already left home, so, as the youngest of the four children, Mary Kay cared for her invalid father while her mother worked long hours as a restaurant manager to support the family.

Mary Kay often told a story of her father wanting potato soup for dinner, and she would always have to call her mother for the recipe.

1

Her mother ended every phone call with, "You can do it." This became Mary Kay's motto, which she would later pass on to others.

Growing up during the Great Depression, Mary Kay learned to be independent at a young age. Her mother often gave her money for shopping, lunch, and a movie. The salesclerks would question Mary Kay's being so young and shopping alone, and she would invite them to call her mother at work.

Mary Kay was very much a product of the Great Depression, a time when people worked hard for little money. To make ends meet during this financial crisis, people recycled their aluminum foil and wrapping paper, and children wore hand-me-downs. Americans learned to live economically and make every penny count. They wasted nothing. Mary Kay also developed these traits of resourcefulness. She could cook, sew, type, and garden, as well as motivate and inspire. Her generation had learned to take care of themselves. While they had ambition and a desire to rise out of poverty, they also had a heart for helping others.

During her school years, Mary Kay was an excellent student. She once wrote about her favorite teacher, Lela B. Scott, who taught fifth grade at Dow Junior High:

> "The thing I remember about her is that she encouraged me to set high goals. She tutored me in extemporaneous speaking and urged me to enter the Texas State Contest in which I won second place. That started me on the road to public speaking which has served me well all my life. I am eternally grateful to her."[2]

In high school, Mary Kay discovered how much she loved being in the spotlight. As a member of her drill team—the Reagan Redcoats— she thrived knowing that all eyes were on the team and on her. Her first experience in the limelight may explain why she loved being part of the extravagant openings at the annual Mary Kay Seminars, the largest event of the year for the Mary Kay sales force.

Mary Kay married shortly after she graduated from high school and had three children: Marylyn, Ben, and Richard. Her husband then went off to fight in World War II and did not come back because he had found someone else. Mary Kay felt like a failure, so much so that it affected her health. Her doctor diagnosed her with crippling arthritis and told her she would soon be an invalid. She recovered, however, and later believed that the stress from her broken marriage brought on these symptoms.

To support her young family, Mary Kay became involved in direct sales and soon discovered that she was a natural saleswoman. She first became acquainted with direct sales when a woman selling parenting books knocked on her door. Mary Kay couldn't afford them, so the saleswoman told her that if she could sell ten sets of books to neighbors and friends, she would give Mary Kay a set for free. Mary Kay not only accomplished this goal, but she also went on to sell even more sets! However, she quickly discovered there was no opportunity for customers to reorder the products, forcing her to continually seek new customers.

Based on this first sales job, Mary Kay soon realized that direct sales could provide her with the income and flexibility she needed to raise her family. She also realized the advantages of products that could be reordered. This understanding prompted her to work for Stanley Home Products, where she achieved success in the late 1930s and the 1940s. Mary Kay learned everything about direct sales through Stanley, which helped her build a solid foundation for starting her own company.

Mary Crowley, who founded Home Interiors and Gifts Inc., became a giant in the world of direct selling, just like Mary Kay. But it was Mary Kay who first recruited Crowley into direct sales, and during a snowstorm, no less! Mary Kay held a Stanley Home Products party for a woman who was a pupil in Mary Crowley's Sunday school class. The two Marys were the only ones who ventured out that night to the hostess's home. As Mary Kay described that evening:

> "The hostess had a one-room apartment that had a baby bed on one wall, a bed on another, a couch on the third wall, and a stove on the fourth . . . I summed up that situation quickly and thought there was no use talking about cleaning house around here—there was no place to do it!
>
> Mary impressed me. Her personality was so terrific. I thought to myself, we might as well just drink the coffee and eat the cake and forget about the Stanley party . . ."[3]

Mary Kay really enjoyed their discussion and could tell that Mary Crowley was a bright and talented woman. As they chatted, Mary Kay discovered that Mary didn't really care about house cleaning, though, and would not be interested in the Stanley products. Turning the conversation in another direction, Mary Kay shared her career story with Mary . . . subtly disclosing how much money she made. Although Mary had a great job as a secretary to the president of a Dallas company and made a good salary for a woman at that time, she was unhappy because she was never around when her children arrived home from school.

On the night of the Stanley party, Mary Crowley was not interested in making a career change. However, she contacted Mary Kay a month later about trying out a part-time career at Stanley. Like Mary Kay, Mary Crowley had a big personality and deep faith. She was always prepared and organized, and her sales were outstanding. Within three weeks, Mary discovered the potential in a direct sales career and quit her full-time job. The two Marys worked together to take Mary Kay's Stanley sales team to the top, bouncing ideas off each other.

Eventually, Mary Kay and Mary quit their jobs at Stanley and moved on to World Gift, another direct sales company that sold home decorative items, but they both were unhappy there. Within a few years of each other, the women left World Gift and each Mary started a successful direct sales company of her own. In recalling their relationship, Mary Kay said, ". . . Mary and I really hit it off because our philosophies were so similar, our ways of thinking so much alike, and we just did well together!"[4]

When Mary Kay first joined World Gift, she became its Houston manager. In just a few years, she was promoted to National Training Director. She had all the responsibilities of this position, but received half the income of her male peers who were at the same managerial level.

At World Gift, Mary Kay often trained men who were then promoted over her. When she asked why this was so, her managers told her that the men had families to support. But, as a single mother, Mary Kay also supported her family. Mary Kay eventually hit the glass ceiling. She often submitted ideas to help improve the workplace, only to be told that she was just thinking like a woman. One day, in 1963, her frustration boiled over, and she resigned from her job at World Gift. She said later that she went home that day and cried. If they had called her to return, she would have gladly gone back. However, they didn't call, and Mary Kay realized she had to move forward with her life. "You learn more from seeing something done incorrectly than seeing it done correctly," she often told me. Although her years at World Gift were frustrating, she used these negative experiences to improve herself and to hone her interpersonal skills.

By 1963, Mary Kay's children had grown up and left home. She needed something to do, so she decided to write a book on selling techniques for women to help those who had sales careers. After all, she had twenty-five years of experience in sales as a top saleswoman. On a legal pad, she made three lists.

1. Good things she'd seen in companies
2. Things that needed to be improved
3. How she would improve things if she had control

While looking at the entries underneath the three lists, it dawned on Mary Kay that she had just put a marketing plan on paper, and she realized that she could put this plan into action. With her background in direct sales and her experience in rising from the ground floor, she knew just what opportunities a direct selling career could provide for those who worked diligently.

Mary Kay's goal wasn't to build a billion-dollar company, though. Her goal was simple: she wanted to help women. The first dimension of her company was based on a desire to provide women in sales with the opportunities she had been denied. Mary Kay also wanted to give women the opportunity to have a fulfilling career and, at the same time, be able to keep their priorities in what she believed was the proper perspective: God first, family second, and career third.

The second dimension of her new company involved her marketing plan: direct sales. After twenty-five years in sales, Mary Kay knew this business offered a woman the ability to determine her own income and working hours. As a young saleswoman, she had wanted a defined career path. She had wanted to know how to get to the next level, but no one would give her a solid answer. As a result, she determined to build a company with a clearly defined ladder of success.

The third dimension of the company would be its product. Mary Kay wanted a product that would generate repeat sales and appeal to women. She knew firsthand the importance of reorders after selling mops and furniture polish as a Stanley Home Products representative.

Mary Kay knew that most women loved cosmetics, and she had been using an excellent skin care line that she discovered in the early 1950s. During one of her Stanley Home parties, she noticed all the guests had perfect complexions. The twenty guests fell between the ages of nineteen to seventy, so their across-the-board flawless skin stood out even more. After the party, Mary Kay found out that every guest was a skin care customer of the hostess. Mary Kay asked to try the products, so the hostess gave her a shoebox full of them. Mary Kay loved the products and continued using them after that party.

As she developed plans to start her own company, Mary Kay knew that these skin care products had not been marketed well, so she decided to spend her life savings to purchase the formulas. She added some glamour and body care items to the lineup, and—with the products she now owned—she started her first business, Beauty by Mary Kay.

Of course, Mary Kay believed that people—her sales force and staff—were the most important asset of her company. She taught that everyone should be treated fairly and with respect. She saw the contribution each person made to the company, and she applauded it. As she often told people, "When the air conditioner stops working during a Texas summer, the most important person in the building is the maintenance man." Mary Kay appreciated the employees who worked at the company's manufacturing plant and distribution centers and would often make visits to these facilities. She would walk up and down the assembly lines and talk to every person, thanking them for their contributions to the company.

One of her favorite illustrations was when she compared her company to a wheel, with employees and sales force members acting as the spokes. Each one supported the wheel and made it move forward. When everyone did their jobs properly, the company made progress, and Mary Kay saw making progress as touching lives.

Women join the Mary Kay sales force as Independent Beauty Consultants. The first tier of sales force management in Mary Kay is that of the Independent Sales Director. Their organizations are called units. The highest level in the sales force is that of the Independent National Sales Director. Their organizations are called areas. In the United States today, the company has more than 300,000 Independent Beauty Consultants, and there are approximately 250 National Sales Directors. These women are extraordinary leaders, and Mary Kay has empowered them to carry on her legacy among the sales force.[5]

Starting this company took a big leap of faith from Mary Kay. In the 1950s and early 1960s, women were not welcome in the executive suite or the boardroom. But she knew many smart and talented women who she believed could achieve great things if given the opportunity. She wanted to give them chances for success that she had been denied. She also wanted to develop a company based on the Golden Rule philosophy, something unheard of in this era. She immediately faced obstacles, the first and biggest of which being the death of her second husband, who died of a heart attack at the breakfast table just one month before the company opened. Mary Kay had only recently remarried, and her new husband had handled the financial and administrative portion of the business because she was the expert in sales and marketing.

When Mary Kay sought professional advice on how to proceed after this tragedy, most experts discouraged her from continuing her venture. Her attorney advised her of how many cosmetic companies go broke every year. Her accountant told her she would never make any money with the commission schedule she proposed. The president of another company told Mary Kay that she might as well sell him the cosmetic formulas as she would go broke within months.

Fortunately, Mary Kay's children believed in her. Her youngest son, Richard—who was twenty at the time—took a substantial pay cut to help her start the business, becoming her co-founder, business partner, and administrator. Ben, Mary Kay's second son, gave her the money in his savings account and later joined the business. Her daughter Marylyn became the first Sales Director.

Beauty by Mary Kay officially opened its doors on Friday, September 13, 1963. Mary Kay chose the historically unlucky day for a very simple reason: it was the day their lease began. She didn't want to waste time or money in getting the business up and running.

To publicize her new company, Mary Kay ran an ad in a Dallas newspaper announcing the grand opening. She had leased a five-hundred-square-foot storefront, which became the office, warehouse, and distribution center. Richard somehow convinced Mary Kay that a bikini-clad model passing out champagne at the door would draw a crowd. The whole idea sounded out of character for Mary Kay, but Richard must have sold this idea with enthusiasm. She went along because she loved her son. The result? The opening drew more men than women, and therefore did not attract Mary Kay's desired clientele.

At the start, Beauty by Mary Kay not only sold skin care and glamour products, but also human-hair wigs. Wigs were popular in the 1960s and retailed anywhere between $100 and $300: much more than the basic Beauty by Mary Kay skin care set, priced at $15.95. Customers could see some sample wigs at a skin care class, and if the customer wanted one, she would go to the Beauty by Mary Kay office to select her wig of choice. The company hired professional stylists to customize wigs for buyers, but stylists didn't always listen to their client's desires, which resulted in many unhappy customers. So, in 1965, Mary Kay discontinued the human-hair wigs.

This proved to be a wise business decision because, once the sales force concentrated solely on skin care, sales increased by $20,000 the very next month.[6] And, true to her thrifty roots, Mary Kay kept the remaining wigs in her inventory and gave them away as prizes for top Consultants.

Mary Kay started her company with nine saleswomen—some of whom were her good friends—and called them Beauty Consultants. In the very early days of the company, Mary Kay personally held many of the "beauty shows" in the homes of her hostesses. However, when potential customers heard that she was also the president, they wondered about the company's stability, so she stepped back and concentrated on training the sales force. One of the first company goals was to recruit and train one hundred quality saleswomen. These first saleswomen were to be a group so prestigious that other women would want to join Beauty by Mary Kay. Within a year, the company achieved this goal.

As the number of saleswomen grew, Mary Kay could not continue to personally train and develop every Beauty Consultant. She and her son Richard recognized that leaders had emerged from the existing Beauty Consultants. Some naturally brought others into the business and trained them. Therefore, the position of Sales Director evolved from the Beauty Consultants. Mary Kay then taught training classes to all new Sales Directors and held monthly meetings for them at the company's Dallas headquarters.

From the beginning, Mary Kay had dreamed of a company that operated on the Golden Rule. Her sincere desire was that every person who was and is a part of the Mary Kay family would live by this rule, not only in their Mary Kay roles, but in their personal lives as well. She always advised others to make every decision based on this rule. Whenever there was a question about how to handle a situation, Mary Kay's advice was to put oneself in the place of the other person and treat that person exactly as one would want to be treated.

When Mary Kay trained her Sales Directors, she would not only speak to them about the Golden Rule's importance; she also presented them with a tiny marble that had the Golden Rule inscribed around the circumference. The idea for the marble came from a motivational speaker who was invited to a Sales Director meeting in the company's early years. During his presentation, the motivational speaker told the group about another company that also practiced the Golden Rule philosophy. To remind their employees of its importance, that company used a marble inscribed with the Golden Rule. Mary Kay was excited about the marble, for while she and her sales force members often discussed the Golden Rule, she felt that a tangible reminder of this creed would be an effective tool. During that meeting, one of the Sales Directors called the marble manufacturer and ordered the first batch of Golden Rule marbles for the company.

Mary Kay gave away thousands of these marbles throughout the company's history. When she did, she would always remind the recipients that life is not a bed of roses without thorns. Whenever they faced a crucial decision, Mary Kay asked them to hold the marble and ask themselves how they could solve the problem by using the Golden Rule philosophy.

Mary Kay's relationship with God was also at the core of her new company. Her life philosophy was, "God first, family second, and career third." Company meetings and meals opened with prayer. She took God as her business partner, and she always gave Him the credit for any success she might have. She wanted her company to not only help women financially, but also emotionally and spiritually. She wove her faith into everything she did: her speeches, her correspondence, and her actions. In her autobiography, Mary Kay insisted, "I believe we found success because God has led us all the way."[7]

Acknowledging God ultimately made a big difference in the company's success. Because of Mary Kay's faith, the sales force developed a strong belief that God would provide and that they could overcome any difficulty.

Mary Kay sincerely believed that the primary purpose of her company was to help people. She often said, "I want all those who come in contact with Mary Kay Inc. to be enriched by their association with us." Whether someone was a part of Mary Kay for one year, ten years, or as a lifetime career, she wanted that person to be able to look back on that time and say, "I was blessed by being a part of Mary Kay."

Beauty by Mary Kay—which in the late 1960s became known as Mary Kay Cosmetics—experienced exponential growth in the late 1960s and 1970s. By the end of 1967, the company had grown to $4,700,000 in sales, touting 2,763 sales force members.[8] When Mary Kay took the company public in 1968, the stock soared. In the public eye, a mystique surrounded Mary Kay and her upstart organization. People took notice and wondered about the secret to her success.

In 1979, Mary Kay and her company were thrust into the national limelight when she was interviewed for the CBS news broadcast *60 Minutes*. The show's producers came to Dallas and met with Mary Kay Cosmetics' corporate executives and Mary Kay to ascertain if she had a story worth telling. However, after that meeting, Mary Kay did not hear from the producers for many months. Then, she received a phone call from *60 Minutes* on a Friday afternoon in May 1979. They told Mary Kay that their production crew would be at the office on Monday morning to film her. When she pointed out that Monday was Memorial Day and that the office would be closed, they decided to film her at home.

True to form, Mary Kay immediately went home and started cleaning. She was a very meticulous housekeeper. She wanted everything to be perfect. Her third husband, Mel, vacuumed while she touched up the baseboards with a can of paint. Unfortunately, Mel knocked over the paint can with the vacuum cleaner, and, although they got the stain out, the smell of turpentine lingered, and the carpet remained squishy. As luck would have it, the *60 Minutes* crew set up their camera right over the spot.

The paint fiasco wasn't the only thing that went awry. In the middle of the interview, Mary Kay heard a noise in the kitchen. She got up to see where the noise had come from, saw water running out of the refrigerator, and realized that the ice maker had broken. She promptly called a plumber and began to explain in her sweet, Southern way that she had an emergency. The plumber refused to make a house call, saying he did not work on Memorial Day. The *60 Minutes* producer then took the phone out of Mary Kay's hand and explained to the plumber that she was with *60 Minutes* at Mary Kay Ash's house filming an interview, and if he didn't come over immediately, they would do an exposé on him! Needless to say, the plumber soon arrived.

On camera, Mary Kay talked about the company's Golden Rule philosophy and her desire that the Mary Kay Cosmetics sales force live with the priorities of God first, family second, and career third. At that point, interviewer Morley Safer asked Mary Kay if she was "using God." Without any hesitation, she replied sincerely, "I hope not. I sincerely hope not. I hope God is using me instead."[9]

In those years, most *60 Minutes* segments exposed negative things about organizations or people, so Mary Kay and her executives were concerned with how the show would present Mary Kay and the company. During the filming for the segment, though, the *60 Minutes* crew had also traveled to Canada to chronicle an event that Mary Kay held for sales force members and their guests. After the meeting ended, the producer shook Mary Kay's hand and told her, "You are really somebody, and this is one of the most enlightened experiences of my career. I have enjoyed working with you." Mary Kay was touched and felt confident about how the show would portray her and the company.

Her intuition was right. Mary Kay Cosmetics was such an ethical company that the show could not find anything negative to report.

Instead, the producers took a whimsical approach. They portrayed a little company in Dallas, headed by a great-grandmother, where the women sang songs, had fun, and sold skin care and cosmetics. The program aired on a Sunday evening in October. The following Monday morning, the phones at Mary Kay headquarters didn't stop ringing. Mail came pouring into the company. Mary Kay Cosmetics became famous across the United States almost overnight. During the next few years, many more women joined the sales force, and sales skyrocketed.

60 Minutes was just the beginning of Mary Kay's national interviews and appearances. In 1981, the editor of *The Saturday Evening Post,* Dr. Cory SerVaas, spotted Mary Kay at the airport and wanted an interview. When she learned that Mary Kay was about to board a plane, SerVaas rushed to the ticket counter and secured a ticket on the same flight in the seat next to Mary Kay.

During the flight, SerVaas asked Mary Kay to share a story that she had never told the media. Mary Kay chose to talk about the brain surgery she underwent before she began Mary Kay Cosmetics. She revealed that, in 1957, when she was the National Training Director for World Gift, she developed a tic in her left eye. The condition worsened, and by 1962 it had spread to the left side of her face and forehead, causing her to twitch several times a minute. As a public speaker and motivator, this tic was very disruptive to her audiences and to her message. Mary Kay recalled that, after she had given what she felt was a powerful speech, people came up to her and said, "Your face didn't seem to twitch as much today!" Mary Kay realized that people could not focus on her words because they only watched her face. She knew something had to be done.

Mary Kay consulted a Dallas neurosurgeon, who diagnosed the condition as a hemifacial spasm and told her the only remedy was surgery. She was referred to Dr. James Gardner of the Cleveland Clinic, who told her if the condition wasn't corrected, it could worsen and affect her other senses, immobilizing her ability to taste, smell, see, and feel. Prior to the introduction of the CT scan in the early 1970s, brain surgery was highly dangerous.[10] But Mary Kay was optimistic, and she thought she would recover in a few days. Instead, she endured an eight-hour operation and was in the hospital for two months. She later said that, without the operation, she would not have been able to start Mary Kay Cosmetics, and her gratitude to Dr. Gardner was immense.

After listening to her story, SerVaas wanted to put Mary Kay on the cover of *The Saturday Evening Post*. Mary Kay happily agreed to send her a photo. However, SerVaas insisted the magazine fly Mary Kay to New York City to be photographed by celebrity photographer Francesco Scavullo. Mary Kay agreed to the photoshoot. Makeup artist John Richardson did her color cosmetics, and she took copious notes. This trip marked the "glamming of Mary Kay." She returned to Dallas a cosmetic queen, and the photos from this magazine cover story became iconic portraits of her at the company headquarters.

From that point forward, Mary Kay's fame continued to grow. She wrote three best-selling books: she published her autobiography, *Miracles Happen: The Life and Timeless Principles of The Founder of Mary Kay Inc.*, in 1981; a book on people management, *Mary Kay on People Management*, in 1984; and a book on balance in life, *You Can Have It All*, in 1995. She also appeared on talk shows such as *The Oprah Winfrey Show* and *The 700 Club* in 1981, *The Late Show with David Letterman* in 1982, and on *Good Morning America*. No matter how much publicity she received, however, Mary Kay stayed the same down-to-earth person she always had been.

In 1995, Skip Hollandsworth at *Texas Monthly* asked Mary Kay for an interview, and she graciously spent time with him. To her dismay, he wrote a scathing piece depicting her totally out of character, and

Mary Kay was very hurt by his vindictive portrayal. A movie titled *Hell on Heels: The Battle of Mary Kay* debuted in 2002, starring Shirley MacLaine as Mary Kay Ash. The movie was somewhat based on Hollandsworth's inaccurate article but had no basis in reality.

In fact, there were some ridiculous scenes in the movie, like when Shirley MacLaine would open a box on her desk containing a mirror in which to admire herself, implying that Mary Kay was obsessed with her looks. After the movie was released, people who toured Mary Kay's office would ask about the box, even though there was no such thing. Of course, Mary Kay believed that she should always look her best—as a cosmetic executive—but she was not vain.

Another laughable scene took place when Shirley MacLaine ran into an elevator to avoid the press. Mary Kay never ran from a reporter. She was always open to meeting with the media. She would quip, "As long as the newspaper spells your name right, that's all that matters." Mary Kay had a message she wanted to communicate: women are wonderful, and they can do great things when given the opportunity.

Choosing Shirley MacLaine to play Mary Kay was an odd casting choice as she and Mary Kay were totally opposite in character. Mary Kay always said that she wanted Dolly Parton to play her if anyone ever made a movie of her life. Ironically, *Texas Monthly* named Mary Kay the "Salesman of the Century" in 1999, five years after Hollandsworth's negative magazine article.

During the 1980s and 1990s, Mary Kay Cosmetics expanded into the global markets, touching lives around the world. At that point, Mary Kay realized that the company needed a larger facility and more staff. In 1995, Mary Kay Inc. moved its headquarters to an impressive building in Addison, Texas. Mary Kay was excited because the building had thirteen floors and thirteen elevators, her lucky number. Sadly, she was unable to enjoy this beautiful building for long, because on February 26, 1996, she suffered a debilitating stroke that left her unable to work.

Even after her stroke, however, Mary Kay loved hearing stories about the women whose lives had been changed because of Mary Kay Inc. She could see that her dream company would continue to touch women's lives even when she no longer led it. She also firmly believed that Mary Kay Inc. had been divinely inspired. Mary Kay spent twenty-five years in direct sales preparing for the day when she would start her own company, one that put God at the helm and that ran its business with the Golden Rule philosophy as its core. Those who worked with her knew this sincere conviction. As Dick Bartlett, Vice Chairman of Mary Kay Inc., observed, "She [Mary Kay] was confident that there was a grand pattern to her life. In the 30 years I knew her, I never saw her waver from her purpose, not once. I invite you to think how many people you've met about whom you'd say the same thing."[11]

Proof of Mary Kay's extraordinary commitment to her goal can be seen in the awards and honors she received during her lifetime:[12]

- Inducted into the Direct Selling Association Hall of Fame in 1976. She also received the Circle of Honor Award in 1989 and the Living Legend Award in 1992 from the Direct Selling Education Foundation.
- Inducted into the Texas Women's Hall of Fame in 1986, the Texas Business Hall of Fame in 1986, and the National Business Hall of Fame in 1996.
- Recipient of the Women of the Century Award from the Women's Chamber of Commerce of Texas in 1999, which honored the state's one hundred most influential women of the twentieth century.
- Featured in Daniel Gross's 1997 book, *Forbes Greatest Business Stories of All Time*, as one of twenty entrepreneurs, and the only woman business leader profiled.

- Named "Salesman of the Century" in 1999 by *Texas Monthly* magazine.
- Posthumously named the "Greatest Female Entrepreneur in American History" by Baylor University in 2003.
- Featured in the 2007 Biography Channel Series "Mary Kay" by *A&E Television Networks*.
- Named one of the one hundred "Women of the Century" by *USA Today* in 2020.

In 1978, Mary Kay also received the Horatio Alger Distinguished American Citizens Award. This award is given annually to notable Americans who live the "rags to riches story"—that is, they are born into poverty, but, through persistence and vision, achieve greatness within their lifetimes. They must be "contemporary role models whose experiences exemplify that opportunities for a successful life are available to all individuals who are dedicated to the principles of integrity, hard work, perseverance and compassion for others."[13]

After receiving this award, Mary Kay became active in the Horatio Alger Association, attending their annual meeting regularly. She would always purchase a table at the gathering, which she shared with Mary Kay sales force members in Washington, D.C., who had to qualify to attend.

Because her fellow award recipients were also her peers, Mary Kay developed many warm friendships among the Association's members. One of the Horatio Alger Association's missions is to inspire teenagers in economically underprivileged high schools to set goals and believe that they can make something of their lives. Mary Kay was often paired with Dave Thomas, founder of Wendy's Hamburgers, to speak at youth events. Dave would ensure that he and Mary Kay would always be seated at a table together during the first dinner of the annual meeting so they could catch up on their lives.

Other recipients with whom Mary Kay developed friendships were Woodrow Wilson "Foots" Clements, Dr. Robert Schuller, Helen Boehm, and Tom L. Harken. Mary Crowley also received the Horatio Alger Award in 1978, in the same year as Mary Kay.

Over the years, Mary Kay had noticed that the number of female-to-male recipients in the Association was lopsided, so she began nominating women for membership. Although she did not nominate Carol Burnett, Mary Kay was thrilled to present the award to the actress in 1988.

Nancy Thomason accompanied Mary Kay to these events and recalls how humbled Mary Kay felt to be part of this group. Instead of making a grand entrance, Mary Kay would quietly enter the awards reception by a side door. As she chatted with the service people, others would notice her and immediately migrate her way. According to Nancy, these exceptional individuals held Mary Kay in high regard. Mary Kay never sought accolades, however, and was never impressed by them. Even though she was invited to many prestigious events, several of which were held at the White House, she rarely attended. Mary Kay was not one to show up just to be seen; there had to be a purpose behind her accepting an engagement.

In the end, Mary Kay always felt that her greatest achievement was the hundreds of thousands of Beauty Consultants worldwide whose lives had been enriched by the Mary Kay opportunity. That is what motivated her, and this was the accomplishment closest to her heart.

2

MARY KAY'S PERSONAL LIFE

Precious treasure and oil are in a wise man's dwelling . . .

PROVERBS 21:20

*My priorities have always been God first, family second,
career third. I have found that when I put my life in this order,
everything seems to work out.*

MARY KAY ASH[1]

When people discover that I worked directly with Mary Kay Ash for
many years, they always ask the same thing: "What was she really like?"
Sales force members often beg me: "Tell a Mary Kay story!" They want
to learn more about how she lived her life outside of the office. What
I can assure them is that Mary Kay's life wasn't all work. She did have
her hobbies, and many stories come to mind involving her pursuits
outside of the office.

FOOD

Cooking and eating go hand-in-hand, and Mary Kay loved them both.
During Mary Kay's childhood, her mother worked long hours manag-
ing a restaurant, so Mary Kay grew up cooking for her invalid father.
As she grew older, collecting cookbooks and recipes became a lifelong

hobby. Mary Kay had a large cookbook collection, and when she tried a recipe, she would write notations in the margins with her ratings or any modifications she made. She especially liked cookie recipes. Every month, she would host debuting Mary Kay Sales Directors within her home, where she would serve them tea and homemade cookies.

Mary Kay's favorite holiday was Thanksgiving. She was thrilled that she had sixteen grandchildren, over thirty great-grandchildren, and even several great-great-grandchildren before she passed away. They filled her house every Thanksgiving, and she loved cooking for them at this special time of year. Her signature dish was her jalapeño cornbread. She cooked two batches: one with jalapeños and one without jalapeños. The regular cornbread she labeled "Tenderfoot," and called it worthless. The other she labeled "The Good Stuff." Mary Kay was frequently asked to make contributions to celebrity cookbooks, and she always submitted her jalapeño cornbread recipe.[2]

Mary Kay and the Sales Directors always shared recipes with each other. In the 1960s, when the Sales Directors would come to Dallas for their monthly meetings, they would have potluck luncheons. On even months, Sales Directors whose last names began with the letters A-L would bring the main dish, and those with last names beginning with the letters M-Z would bring the side dishes. On odd months, they would switch. Mary Kay knew that these women were excellent cooks, and she always wanted to create a Mary Kay cookbook. This dream was realized in 1985 when the company produced *Cooking with Mary Kay*, in which she included many of her favorite recipes.

Another thing I learned while working with Mary Kay is that she liked her food spicy—the hotter, the better! She carried a product in her purse called "Texas Gunpowder," which was made of dried and ground-up jalapeños. If she thought her food in a restaurant was bland, she would pull out her "gunpowder" and sprinkle her dish liberally. If someone who was unacquainted with her eating habits ate with Mary

Kay, she would sweetly offer to share her spice that "made food taste better." The unsuspecting victims—who had seen Mary Kay liberally sprinkle her food with the powder—would do likewise, and Mary Kay always got a kick out of watching their faces when they took their first bites. There was a bit of an imp in Mary Kay!

Because she liked her food so hot, Mexican food was her favorite. She was good friends with Anita Martinez, the daughter of the founder of El Fenix, a Dallas Tex-Mex restaurant. The two would occasionally meet for lunch, and Mary Kay regularly patronized El Fenix for their Wednesday enchilada special.

Mary Kay often amazed people with how hot she could take her food. When having dinner with the Mary Kay Operations staff in Monterrey, Mexico, small dishes of pea-sized green peppers—called habaneros—were set out on the table. The Mexico staff advised Mary Kay against eating the peppers, as they were *very* hot. Once they ate their peppers, everyone chased the spice with bread, chips, and lots of drinks. Mary Kay ate the peppers as if they were peanuts or popcorn.

Mary Kay also liked foods that fell under the classification of "home cooking": fried chicken, a hot dog, or a good hamburger would always satisfy her. One time, after a sumptuous banquet at a fancy hotel in Hong Kong, she saw the Golden Arches from her hotel window and sent Nancy Thomason out for a hamburger.

Like many women, Mary Kay was conscious of her weight. For this reason, she would bring her lunch to work every day, which usually consisted of a salad and a piece of jalapeño cornbread. Although Mary Kay talked about diets quite often, she did not practice what she preached. She tried many different diet plans, and her weight often fluctuated. She joked that when she was a baby, she went straight into a size fourteen dress. She would often quip, "There are three sizes of women: small, medium, and luscious." At one point, her doctor put her on a salt-free diet. As soon as Mary Kay got into the office, she handed me the sheets of information he had given her and said, "Put these somewhere I won't see them. I'd rather die than follow this diet."

On Mary Kay Inc.'s fortieth anniversary, the company commissioned a porcelain likeness of Mary Kay as part of the prizes for that year's Seminar. When Mary Kay saw the prototype, she liked it, but she wanted the final version to be "a little thinner."

Mary Kay also had a sweet tooth. She kept her favorite candy, a Mr. Goodbar, in her desk at all times.[3] If dessert was pre-set at any of the many luncheons and dinners she attended, she would always eat it first. When one of the vice presidents asked her why she did this, she told him, "In case there's a fire."

Mary Kay was not a proponent of exercise and did not incorporate it into her daily routine. When it came up in conversations, she would say that she was a member of EA: Exercise Anonymous. "If you feel the urge to exercise, call me and I will talk you out of it," she told those around her. For Christmas one year, her son Richard gave her a treadmill. It didn't last a week before she sent it away. After Mary Kay passed away, Nancy Thomason and I were given the responsibility of going through her house and organizing her things; we discovered a closet full of dated exercise equipment. We both agreed that we never once saw Mary Kay use any of it!

GARDENING

Gardening was another great love of Mary Kay's, so much so that she incorporated her love of nature into the home that she and her husband Mel built together. Mary Crowley, whom Mary Kay had met in her early career as a Stanley Home Products dealer, was responsible for Mary Kay meeting Mel Ash; the pair married in 1966, three years after she founded the company. Mel was friends with Mary, and he once asked her, "Don't you know anyone like you that you could introduce me to?" She told him that she did—and that someone was Mary Kay.

Once Mary Kay and Mel married, they decided to build a home and started collecting pictures of houses they liked. When they compared their files, they discovered that they both wanted a round house, so they built the very first round house in Dallas. Mary Kay gardened in a circular atrium in the middle of the house. Every weekend, she took care of her plants. She had a green thumb, and plants flourished in the atrium's humidity. One of Mary Kay's favorites was a kalanchoe, or widow's-thrill, given to her from the funeral of the very first Mary Kay Sales Director, who had passed away from cancer. The plant multiplied greatly in her atrium and became a kind of memorial. Mary Kay took many cuttings from this plant to pass along to others in remembrance of this beloved Sales Director.

Even when plants didn't flourish under her green thumb, Mary Kay found ways to keep them green. She tried to keep two evergreen plants in large pots on her front porch, but they kept dying because they didn't get enough sunlight. When I was at her house one day, I noticed that they looked as if they were thriving. "Mary Kay, you've gotten two plants to live here!" I commented, only to have her explain how she had solved this problem: she bought a can of green aerosol paint and sprayed them all over. They never died again!

Mary Kay always wanted a beautiful yard and used her ingenuity to keep her flora blooming. She had the most perfect tulips and daffodils in the spring that came up early and lasted throughout the season. They were so lovely that neighbors out for a stroll would often stop to ask her security officers what kind of fertilizer she used. She did have a secret, but it was not fertilizer: when it came time for tulips to bloom, she would plant artificial tulips after dark. They looked so real, though, that everyone who saw them commented on their beauty.

As the company grew, Mary Kay travelled nearly every weekend for events, interviews, and speaking engagements, so she had less time for gardening. After it became too much work for her to keep her atrium plants under control, she turned the atrium into an indoor patio. The last time I was there, she had covered tables and pedestals with beautiful orchids that thrived in that humid, sunlit area.

READING

Reading was another favorite pastime of Mary Kay's. She once told me that reading was one of the most delightful pastimes of her entire life. When she had leisure time, she enjoyed selecting a good book from her library, curling up in a comfortable chair, and reading. Mary Kay liked to read mystery stories and had quite a collection. She didn't have a favorite author; she just liked a good mystery and enjoyed trying to figure out "whodunnit" before the author revealed the answer. As a girl, one of her favorite books was *Little Women* by Louisa May Alcott.

DOGS

Everyone who worked closely with Mary Kay soon learned that she was a dog lover, and her pets brought her much joy. She jokingly called them her "fur people." When the company was in its early days and had a tiny staff, she would bring Monet, her gray poodle, with her to the office. He was not a favorite among the staff, however, as he tended to mark his territory—inside!

After Monet died, Mary Kay owned an adorable white poodle named Gigi, who was cute to look at, but also mean. When Mary Kay would host the new Sales Directors at her home, they would "ooh" and "aah" over Gigi. Those who reached down to pet her, though, discovered she had a very threatening growl, and pulled back immediately.

Mary Kay's last fur person was a happy-go-lucky Bichon Frise named Brie; he kept Mary Kay laughing. Once, when she and her protective service officers had a cookout on her patio, she broke off a bit of hamburger to feed to Brie. He came running toward her, jumped up, and took the remaining hamburger from her hand, leaving Mary Kay with the tiny bite intended for him. Mary Kay got the giggles over this and his other antics. After Mary Kay's death, Nancy Thomason took Brie home with her, and he lived a full and contented life tormenting Nancy's older, more serious Bichon Frise.

PAINTING

In the late 1970s, Mary Kay decided she wanted to paint. After reading the story of Anna Mary Robertson Moses, or "Grandma Moses," Mary Kay was so inspired that she went to the art supply store and purchased the materials she needed to paint. One Sunday afternoon, she told Mel that she was going to "paint her masterpiece." Mary Kay painted several pictures before she tired of this new hobby. Two of these were of girls amid flowers, as seen from the back, since Mary Kay did not want to attempt to paint their faces. Some of her paintings are displayed during Seminar in the company's corporate offices.

HUMOR

When those who knew her well talk about Mary Kay, her wonderful sense of humor always comes up. In her book *You Can Have It All*, she dedicates a whole chapter to humor, advising readers that "many people fail to see the humorous side of life, and consequently endure unnecessary stress. Oftentimes, situations that border on catastrophic are actually rather amusing—later. Admittedly, you might have to look hard for something funny, but, if you do, chances are you'll find it."[4]

As one example of what she meant, from 1971 to the early 2000s, pink Mary Kay Peterbilt trucks crossed the highways across the United States carrying company products. Mary Kay was very proud of this fleet and she loved to meet with the employees who drove the rigs. Although they received a considerable amount of teasing about the color of their trucks, the drivers delighted in the attention they received from Mary Kay and other truckers on the road. At one meeting with the transportation employees, Mary Kay announced that the drivers would soon be wearing new pink jumpsuits with the company logo on the back, which prompted an uproar of protest from the drivers. She then broke into a wide grin, and with a twinkle in her eye, admitted that the company had no such plans. She had simply wanted to see their reactions. It was just one of the many practical jokes she loved pulling on people.

Mary Kay also knew how to take a tense situation and make a joke out of it, putting everyone at ease. More than four thousand people could testify to this aspect of her personality based on an incident in 1994. Mary Kay had just undergone rotator cuff surgery and had not recovered the full use of her arm by the annual Seminar in August. To make the best of the situation, she had slings made to match every one of her onstage outfits. She was to give a speech in Hall A of the Kay Bailey Hutchison Convention Center, and the backstage crew had wired her for the presentation. Because the staff always liked Mary Kay to make dramatic entrances, she was driven onstage in a white golf cart that, of course, matched her white suit.

Nancy Thomason stood at the front of the stage, watching the audience. When Mary Kay stood up, everyone gasped. Nancy whirled around to see what was wrong and saw that Mary Kay's skirt had fallen down and hung around her ankles. The company's Senior Vice President of Sales, who was to introduce her at this event, was standing next to her. Cavalierly, he reached down, pulled up her skirt and zipped it. Undeterred by this catastrophe, Mary Kay walked to the podium and said, "Now, how was that for an entrance?"

This was the second time that Mary Kay's skirt had fallen to her feet at an inopportune moment. While attending the wedding of a prominent Dallas newscaster and friend, Mary Kay went to hug a rather tall newsman for whom she had great affection. As she reached up, her skirt went down. Her immediate thought was, "I have just lost my skirt in front of all of these Dallas reporters." It is a testimony to the respect that the Dallas community had for Mary Kay Ash that the media did not report one word of this, much to her relief.

On Mary Kay's last trip to New York City, she appeared on *CBS This Morning*. Mary Kay had a policy to never reveal her age, especially to reporters. If they asked, she would answer, "A woman who will tell her age will tell anything." After the interview, Paula Zahn came up to Mary Kay and asked, "Really, Mary Kay, what is your age?" Without missing a beat, Mary Kay replied, "Well, Paula, what is your weight?" Paula then dropped the question for good.

Mary Kay attended so many company trips, luncheons, and dinners that many of her witticisms are recounted by those who sat next to her. In Elite Executive National Sales Director Emeritus Doretha Dingler's book, *In Pink*, she recalls the very first trip planned for the top echelon of the sales force, the National Sales Directors.[5] Of course, because of their status, the women expected an elegant experience. However, the chosen venue turned out to be a hunting lodge called Tan-Tar-A, in Osage Beach, Missouri, on the Lake of the Ozarks. I have heard those who went on this trip describe their uneasiness when they boarded small puddle-jumper planes en route to their destination and found chained prisoners transported on the flights as well.

The lodge was huge, and the staff and Nationals were housed in cabins. To get to their meetings, they rode from their cabins to the lodge in golf carts. Members of the Mary Kay sales force love to dress up, so they had come on the trip with all their finery, high heels, and jewels. What a contrast they must have made to the typical lodge guest.

Most Mary Kay Inc. trips involve a blending of business and fun, and this one was no exception. On the first morning after the group arrived, the women attended the kick-off meeting. During the opening remarks, Mary Kay's shoulders suddenly started shaking, and Doretha could tell she was trying to hold back her laughter. Of course, the speaker stopped what he was saying, and everyone turned to Mary Kay. As Doretha describes the scene: "Mary Kay's expressive eyes were filled with laughter-induced tears by the time she explained herself . . . she lost it when she looked up to where there should be chandeliers and saw instead exposed pipes and beams in the cavernous ceiling after we'd been flown in on planes carrying prisoners and transported in all our finery via rustic golf carts. All of this had just suddenly seemed hysterically funny to her."[6] Mary Kay Inc. trips were never again hosted at hunting lodges.

Those sitting by Mary Kay at events often experienced her wit. Tim Danforth, husband to Senior National Sales Director Emeritus Pat Danforth, recalls an incredibly formal ceremonial dinner they attended with Mary Kay in Hong Kong in 1987.[7] That night, the meal was a presentation of Peking Duck, and the waiter made quite a production about giving Mary Kay a mallet to break the ceramic around the duck. As they were leaving, Tim asked Mary Kay, "Did you enjoy the dinner?" to which she retorted, "Just give me a hamburger."

On another occasion, Mary Kay was seated at the head table next to Senior National Sales Director Emeritus Wilda DeKerlegand.[8] Mary Kay commented on how she loved French bread, and she had enjoyed it so much that there were crumbs all over her collar. Wilda noticed a reporter approaching them from across the room and alerted Mary

Kay about the accumulation of crumbs. She leaned close to Wilda and said, "Blow, baby, blow."

When National Sales Director Emeritus Kendra Crist Cross was seated at the head table with Mary Kay at a leadership luncheon, one of the waiters dropped a tray of glassware, causing quite a commotion.[9] Mary Kay looked at Cross and said, "One of my Nationals just dropped a setting in her diamond ring."

Executive National Sales Director Emeritus Arlene Lenarz says that Mary Kay had a zest for life and didn't take herself seriously.[10] She was almost childlike in her enjoyment of adventure. Mary Kay was game for anything, whether it be snowmobiling or camel riding. On one company trip to the Middle East, Arlene and her husband Dick rode a camel next to the one Mary Kay rode. As they slowly lumbered along, Mary Kay turned to Arlene's husband and said, "I'll race you."

Mary Kay was adept at using her sense of humor to help calm those around her. Nan Stroud remembers the year that she was the number one Sales Director. Mary Kay came to Greenville, South Carolina, that January to honor Nan's unit, and before going to Mary Kay's hotel, Nan wanted to take Mary Kay to her home that sat on a mountainside. However, when they pulled up to the driveway, they saw firetrucks. Nan's house was on fire! Mary Kay wanted to be there for Nan, so she trudged up that mountain in her high heels and full-length coat. One of Nan's neighbors, who had been out fishing, came by in his old jalopy and asked if there was anything he could do. Nan asked him if he could take Mary Kay to her hotel. On the way to the hotel, he kept apologizing about his appearance. "Well," Mary Kay said, "you probably feel better than I do in this girdle."[11]

One of my favorite stories about Mary Kay's sense of humor occurred when Mary Kay, Nancy Thomason, Randall Oxford—the company's Public Relations Director in the 1990s—and I were at lunch. Because Mary Kay was passionate about finding a cure for cancer, she subscribed to newsletters that discussed the disease, many of which contained articles on nutrition. Before lunch, Mary Kay brought up the topic of eating healthy. When the waitress came, Mary Kay told us to order first. Since Nancy, Randall, and I had just received a lecture on nutrition, we ordered turkey sandwiches and a salad. Mary Kay then turned to the waitress and said, "I'll have a cheeseburger, French fries, and a chocolate shake," and looked at us with a big grin on her face. To make us feel even more duped, when her shake came, she slurped it with a twinkle in her eye.

As Vice President of Sales Promotion, one of Dale Alexander's roles was to introduce Mary Kay at company events. At a special banquet one night in Bermuda, the top echelon of the National Sales Directors and corporate executives were seated at the head table. As emcee, Dale introduced the head table in ascending order, but somehow, he forgot to introduce Mary Kay.

During the meal, he approached Mary Kay to discuss the program, and Mary Kay smiled at him the whole time he spoke. When he was finished, he asked, "Do you have any questions?" She said, "I do have just one. Do you think you forgot to do something tonight?" Dale answered that he couldn't think of anything. She then told him, "I thought that perhaps you forgot to introduce me." She laughed when she said this, as she and Dale had a very warm relationship. Dale kept apologizing and immediately went to the podium and jokingly referenced his omission.

The next morning at breakfast, Dale again apologized to Mary Kay. "That's okay," she said. "For years, when you have introduced me, you have said, 'We all know that this is a person who really needs no introduction.'" A few days later, back in Dallas, Dale was scheduled to introduce Mary Kay at another event. Dale asked her if she was ready.

When she said she was, he told her, "I will go and introduce you now." To which she joked, "Oh, you still do that?"

Mary Kay was also keen on using humor in her speeches. One of her favorite quips was a quote by Sophie Tucker that she always recited with that twinkle in her eye:

> "From birth to age eighteen, a girl needs good parents.
> From eighteen to thirty-five, she needs good looks.
> From thirty-five to fifty-five, she needs a personality.
> And I am here to tell you that, from fifty-five on,
> what she needs is cash."

3

MARY KAY'S TYPICAL DAY

Commit your work to the Lord,
and your plans will be established.

PROVERBS 16:3

Because I have a fetish about starting each day with a
clean desk, I take home whatever is left when I leave in
the afternoon and do it at night or early in the morning
of the next day so that when I arrive at the office,
everything is finished from the day before.

MARY KAY ASH[1]

One question I am frequently asked is, "What was Mary Kay's typical day like?" The one-word answer would be productive. Mary Kay would always say that she was a workaholic and proud of it! She found work rewarding, for she felt that her God-given mission was to help women.

Mary Kay would rise at 5:00 a.m. every morning. When she was raising her three children and building her Stanley business, she had to find a way to increase her productivity. One of her solutions was to get up early, and she continued this habit throughout her lifetime. She called her early rising habit the "Five O'Clock Club," and she often encouraged others to join her.

In Mary Kay's experience, "Three early risings make an extra day." She discovered that getting up early allowed her to accomplish in one hour what might normally take her three. She would do her household chores tirelessly during those early hours. At 8:30 a.m., she would work on something beneficial for her business and would only take a thirty-minute lunch break. Mary Kay learned to shorten unnecessary phone calls and interruptions just as if she had been working a full-time job for someone else and had a boss looking over her shoulder. She kept a three-minute timer at her desk, as well as a doorbell chime. When she had trouble getting someone off the phone, she would ring her chime and say, "That must be the doorbell. I will talk to you later."

Mary Kay was also an expert at organization. As head of the company, she often found much work piled on her desk at the end of the day; when she left the office at night, she took unfinished work home in her pink tote bag. Mary Kay left her desk completely clear of any work. The next morning, when she got up early, she tackled what was in her pink bag. She would dictate from home and had her own special phone—just like the President of the United States has a special phone that connects to the Pentagon—that connected to a recorder on my desk. When I arrived at the office, I usually found a day's work already lined up for me. Mary Kay also wrote handwritten notes and planned out her day. When she arrived at the office, she would plop the contents of her pink tote bag on my desk to either complete or distribute. Her desk was always neat; mine was always messy.

Next, she would go into her office with her "Six Most Important Things I Must Do Today" list in her hand. As a master of getting things done, she frequently shared this organizational concept with others, and in time, Mary Kay Inc. produced notepads of these blank lists for the entire sales force to use. According to Mary Kay, she got the idea from the story of Ivy Lee, a productivity consultant and public relations pioneer in the early 1900s who called on Charles Schwab, President of the Bethlehem Steel Corporation. Lee told Schwab that he could increase Schwab's efficiency and sales if Lee spent just fifteen minutes with each of his executives. Mr. Schwab asked, "How much will it cost me?" Mr. Lee said, "Nothing. Unless it works."[2]

So, each day for the next three months, Mr. Lee went into each executive's office at the end of day and helped the executives make a list of the six most important things to do for the next day. Schwab and his executives would order the list together. If the executives didn't finish their lists that day, they would put the unfinished items at the top of their lists for the next day. Three months later, Mr. Schwab was so impressed with the results that he sent Lee a check for $35,000.[3] When Mary Kay heard of Lee's idea, she got excited and immediately began using it herself.

On top of all the paperwork, Mary Kay's days were jam-packed with phone calls, meetings, and appointments. However, she kept her door open when she wasn't in meetings or eating lunch, and staff could pop in and out of her office without an appointment. No matter how busy she was, Mary Kay always had time to visit with sales force members when they came to the office. Mary Kay valued her sales force. She could relate to them because her own career began in sales, and she knew how challenging it could be. I often said that Mary Kay had "sales force radar." She seemed to sense any sales force members in the building and would come out of her office to greet them. In her heart, she was always a salesperson.

Mary Kay modeled a great work ethic. She lived by the adage, "Work will win where wishing won't." When she was a young girl, her mother would tell her, "Much good work is lost for the lack of a little more." Mary Kay never forgot this saying and worked tirelessly on behalf of women. When interviewers would ask her what her goal was, I would often hear her say, "If just one more woman today discovers how great she really is, how much God-given talent she has, it will be a great day."

No job was too little or unimportant for Mary Kay, including tending to the office plants. She loved plants and often checked the plants in our offices to see if they needed watering. If they were dry, she would take them to the sink and drown them, much to the dismay of our plant experts. She would then pull off the dead leaves. She would also take the sponges from the coffee bar home and wash them. At work, she made her own coffee, her own tea, and her own lunch.

After Mary Kay's husband Mel passed away in 1980, the company hired a protective team for Mary Kay. This team was responsible for driving her to the office and other places. She refused at first, so her security officers would sit in front of her house, wait for her to leave, and then follow her. Mary Kay always thought it was great fun to try and lose them. When a light turned yellow, she would slow down as if to stop, but would instead race through at the last minute and leave her security behind. Mary Kay would even sneak out of the house. One of her friends would call her to see if she would like to get a hot dog (a favorite meal of hers), and she would leave by the sliding patio door and meet him on the corner. At one point, her son Richard helped her to see how serious her behavior was. Mary Kay no longer raced through yellow lights, but she also would not let the security detail drive her. She wanted to maintain her independence.

What finally persuaded Mary Kay to let her officers drive her was the gasoline crisis in the mid-1980s. Gas station lines were long, and prices were high. Ever-practical and economical, Mary Kay came out of her house one morning and said to Nancy Thomason, "Are we ready to go?" Nancy assumed that they were to drive together, and that was that.

Even after she began letting others drive her, Mary Kay's passion for haste did not diminish. One day, when Nancy was driving Mary

Kay, she informed Nancy, "You are going to have to talk to the new officer." All kinds of thoughts began flowing through Nancy's mind! Mary Kay then said to her, "He always goes the speed limit. When he comes to a stop sign, he always stops, even when no one is around."

Nancy responded, "I can't tell him to break the law." Of course, Mary Kay then saw the absurdity of her request and started laughing. "Well," she said, "you can tell him to hurry up."

Another time, Nancy was waiting for Mary Kay at the airport. One of the officers was to drive her that morning. When they pulled up, Mary Kay was in the driver's seat and the officer sat in the passenger seat. He wasn't driving fast enough for Mary Kay, so she had had him pull over and she took the wheel.

As Mary Kay developed her skills as a saleswoman and motivator, she learned the value of reading inspirational and motivational books. When she was just beginning her career in sales and found herself struggling, she read *Think and Grow Rich* by Napoleon Hill. She credited this book with turning her career around. When Mary Kay found a motivational book that she liked, she would often suggest it to our sales force. In fact, when I began my employment, there was a recommended list of books on sales and motivation for the sales force. As the times changed, Mary Kay started listening to educational cassettes in her car, even before cassette decks were built into cars. She kept a cassette player in the front seat next to her and listened on her drive to and from work.

Mary Kay also used the cassette player to listen to tapes that sales force members would send her in place of writing letters. Some of these tapes were quite lengthy. Her staff always thought, "Who would listen to these?" as many were travelogues of the sender's life. But Mary Kay always listened. After listening, she would respond with a letter. She once received a cassette tape from a blind Beauty Consultant, and the two began a "cassette" relationship. Mary Kay would record a message, mail it to the Beauty Consultant, and later receive an answer from her blind friend. Over time, with Mary Kay's encouragement, this woman rose to the level of Sales Director.

No matter the day of the week and how busy she was at work, however, Mary Kay tried to live for God. In the top drawer of her desk, she kept this prayer:

> O Lord, grant that each one who has to do anything with me today may be happier for it. Let it be given me each hour today what I shall say. Grant me the wisdom of a loving heart that I may say the right thing. Help me to enter into the mind of everyone who talks with me, and keep me alive to the feelings of each one present. Give me a quick eye for little kindnesses, that I may be ready in doing them, and graciously receiving them. Give me a quick perception of the feelings and needs of others, and make me eager-hearted in helping them.—*AUTHOR UNKNOWN*

4

MARY KAY THE TEACHER

She opens her mouth with wisdom, and the teaching of kindness is on her tongue.

PROVERBS 31:26

I believe that each of us has God-given talents within us waiting to be brought into fruition.

MARY KAY ASH[1]

Mary Kay was a motivator and trainer throughout her career in direct sales. Her teachings were centered on how to balance one's life and reach success. She always said that the three best ways to teach were: 1) by example, 2) by example, and 3) by example. "Tell them how, show them how, let them show you they know how," was common advice that she would give to the Mary Kay sales leadership. Mary Kay was a hands-on teacher.

She also knew the importance of repetition. Mary Kay frequently taught on the same topics in her speeches, articles, and one-on-one communications, and she used catchy phrases that could be repeated by the sales force. Many of these phrases are not original to Mary Kay, but she used them to make an impression. Those listed below—and many others—are still part of the Mary Kay culture today:

"The speed of the leader is the speed of the gang."

"What would you do right now if you knew you could not fail?"

"Love your people to success."

"Become a member of the DIN-DIN Club: Do it now! Do it now!"

"God first, family second, and career third. In that order, everything works; out of that order, nothing works."

"If you help enough people get what they want, you will get what you want."

"The faintest ink is better than the most retentive memory."

"We all fail forward to success."

Mary Kay taught her sales force and staff so many life lessons; one could never cover them all. The few lessons featured in this chapter have impressed me the most or are mentioned frequently by others who were exposed to her tutelage. Mary Kay practiced what she preached. In looking at her life, one finds a blueprint for living.

LIVE YOUR LIFE WITH THE PRIORITIES OF GOD FIRST, FAMILY SECOND, CAREER THIRD.

Mary Kay's priorities changed the lives of so many women in the sales force. These priorities drew Elite Executive National Sales Director Emeritus Emily McLaughlin to the company when she joined Mary Kay in January 1971.[2]

Emily had heard many good things about the company, but she couldn't believe they were all true. When she was invited to Seminar, she went to Dallas with a skeptical attitude. Although she was impressed with the top Sales Directors' speeches, when Mary Kay spoke, Emily was enthralled by her stories and personality. Mary Kay explained how to live out the company's priorities with detailed examples.

Hearing Mary Kay speak marked a turning point in Emily's life. She came home, sat down with her husband and three boys, and told them, "Mom is going to start building her own business. This business will be built on God first, then on our family, and then on my career. You are going to help me build my business. We are going to do it by the Golden Rule." She then explained the Golden Rule to her young sons.

Because Mary Kay encouraged the sales force to build their businesses around their faith, Emily felt comfortable in doing so. "She gave me permission to use my faith in my business." Mary Kay taught Emily that it was okay to pray at company events, and Emily followed this example when she held her own meetings. Emily believed that putting God first in her business was an influencing factor in her success.

Emily was also impressed with Mary Kay's belief that family should come second. Every time Mary Kay met Emily, Mary Kay would ask about Emily's family. When Emily's mother was diagnosed with cancer, Emily would drive eight hours once a month to visit and care for her. Mary Kay knew this and called Emily periodically to check in on her and her mother.

National Sales Director Emeritus LaQueta McCollum-Fisher was once in Mary Kay's office when Mary Kay received a call from a Sales Director who was having problems with her husband.[3] LaQueta heard Mary Kay tell this Sales Director, "You need to get your relationship with your husband right and then worry about your career."

National Sales Director Emeritus Nan Stroud also knew about Mary Kay's sincerity in caring about the families of the sales force. When Nan became pregnant with a much-anticipated child, Mary Kay said to her, "I want you to understand that the most important thing you can do is take care of yourself and your baby." When Nan's son Les was born, he didn't sleep much, and neither did Nan. She dropped out of the top ten Sales Directors that year. At Seminar, Mary Kay told Nan, "You are doing what you are supposed to do. Don't be down about your production. Take care of your baby." Nan felt so accepted, and Mary Kay made it easier for Nan to cope with her disappointment.

Kendra Crist Cross credits Mary Kay with helping her keep her work/life balance using the weekly plan sheet. These sheets were available to all sales force members on the consultant order form and displayed one week at a time divided by hours. Beauty Consultants were asked to fill one out each week with just their Mary Kay activities and turn in the sheets to their Sales Directors. Kendra developed her own system for her weekly plan sheet. She would put her spiritual time in yellow, her family time in blue, non-earning career activities in pink, and her earning activities in green. When she looked at her plan sheet, Kendra would ask herself, "Is my life in balance?" She might think it was, but her weekly plan sheet always showed the reality.

Today, some people feel that Mary Kay's priorities and teachings are outdated, but Mary Kay understood that a woman's priorities were important to her. As she affirmed, "My priorities have always been God first, family second, career third. I have found that when I put my life in this order, everything seems to work out . . . God was my first priority early in my career when I was struggling to make ends meet; through the failures and successes I have experienced since then, my faith has remained unshaken."[4]

CONDUCT YOUR BUSINESS AND YOUR LIFE WITH INTEGRITY.

Anyone who knew Mary Kay knew she was a woman of integrity. She set a high standard for herself, her company, and those who associated with Mary Kay Inc. In the early years, when the Sales Directors met in Dallas, Mary Kay would instill within them the ethical basis for building their teams and expected them to pass these principles on to their unit members. As the company grew and these meetings in Dallas were replaced with an annual Leadership Conference and director meetings at Seminar, Mary Kay began to hear about unethical behavior among the sales force, which deeply disturbed her.

Mary Kay asked Elite Executive National Sales Director Emeritus Mickey Ivey to help her with this problem because Mickey had always been known as a woman of integrity among the sales force.[5] When Mary Kay heard there was confusion about what she meant by building a Mary Kay business on the Golden Rule, she asked Mickey to give a speech addressing these concerns at an upcoming National Sales Director meeting, telling her, "We must combat this now." At that time, Mickey had some serious health problems and told Mary Kay that she did not feel capable to take on the assignment. But Mary Kay was adamant: "I have chosen you. I believe you can do it. I need you do to this, Mickey." And Mickey did. She worked on her speech with more diligence than she had given to any of her other speeches, and she shared Mary Kay's heart and the founding principles of Mary Kay Inc.

Brad Glendening, the company's Executive Vice President, General Counsel, and Corporate Secretary, loved to tell others about his job interview with Mary Kay in 1980. A trial lawyer trained to win at all costs, Brad arrived at the Mary Kay Inc. headquarters sporting a frizzy hairdo and cocky attitude that didn't conform to the corporate lawyer look. To his surprise, Mary Kay didn't seem to notice. She was gracious and asked him personal questions to get to know him. At the end of the interview, she told him, "We do what's right here at Mary Kay. Try never to forget that." Brad was stunned and wondered how that would work, but he soon discovered that, when Mary Kay Inc. was wrong or had made a mistake, the company always took responsibility and worked to correct the situation.

Mary Kay was adamant that the sales force build their businesses with integrity, and that included keeping their promises. Senior National Sales Director Emeritus Sue Kirkpatrick once earned a

$5,000 shopping trip to Dallas for herself and her family that included a bird's eye helicopter tour of the city. However, the tour was canceled due to fog that day.[6] Instead, the company made arrangements for Sue and her family to be picked up in a Rolls-Royce. Mary Kay joined Sue for lunch on the shopping tour and the two spent the afternoon together.

As the Kirkpatrick family prepared to leave Dallas, they learned that Mary Kay was still concerned about Sue's children not getting their helicopter ride. Mary Kay then made special arrangements to have a pilot meet the family at a heliport and take them soaring over Dallas. Sue was touched that Mary Kay cared enough about her children to ensure that they wouldn't be disappointed.

Sue also recalls that, on the first time she sat next to Mary Kay at a luncheon, she told Mary Kay about some people who she believed were not building their businesses the "Mary Kay Way." Mary Kay listened intently, and then said, "I have learned that all you send into the lives of others comes back into your own, good and bad." The message that Sue took away from this encounter was, "You don't have to be the Mary Kay police. Concentrate on doing things the right way and trust God to work out the consequences for those who are not conducting themselves the right way. They might not pay for it in their businesses, but they will pay for it in some other area of their lives."

Senior National Sales Director Emeritus Phyllis Pottinger remembers when she saw Mary Kay keep a promise.[7] In 1985, when Mary Kay was building her pink mansion, she had promised a group of Sales Directors that they could tour her new house; unfortunately, it wasn't ready by the time of the scheduled tour. Instead, they had their reception in Mary Kay's round house, and she gave them a tour there. The next afternoon, Mary Kay took the Sales Directors on a tour of her unfinished home—which Phyllis believes was a bonus tour—because Mary Kay did not want them to be disappointed.

MAKE ME FEEL IMPORTANT.

What made Mary Kay special in the eyes of so many is that she lived by this philosophy: "Pretend every single person has a sign around his or her neck that says, 'Make me feel important.'" Mary Kay often said that this was the greatest piece of advice she had ever received. When most people share their memories of Mary Kay, they recall her treating them as if they were the only person in the room with her.

When Mary Kay looked back at her own career, there were moments of disappointment in her life when she told herself, "If I am ever in that position, I will treat people differently." One of the first was when she was a young saleswoman and was awarded a trip to visit the company's headquarters and meet with the president in his home. The company was headquartered in Boston, Massachusetts, over seventeen hundred miles away from Texas. Flying was expensive and rare at that time, so the winners traveled by bus. Mary Kay described this trip as horrendous because the bus broke down several times.

Once they arrived, their group was given a tour of the plant, which Mary Kay said was nice, but it was not the reason for a prolonged bus trip. When the group was finally taken to the president's home, they were only permitted to tour his rose garden, and the president never deigned to meet them in person. This experience was such a letdown for Mary Kay, and it inspired her to always take the time to meet with Sales Directors or any group who came to Dallas. She ensured the company rolled out the red carpet (literally) during special events, such as at Seminar and training meetings.

Before Mary Kay launched her own company, she attended an all-day seminar and was so anxious to shake hands with a sales manager who had delivered an inspiring speech that she stood in line for three hours to meet him. When it was Mary Kay's turn to meet the man, he never even looked at her; instead, he kept looking over her shoulder to check the length of the line. Mary Kay knew that he was probably tired, but so was she. She had stood in line for hours to meet him. She decided that if she were ever in a position where people wanted to meet her, she would give them her undivided attention, no matter how tired she felt. Mary Kay's commitment to that principle is one of the things that people especially remember about her: she was willing to stand in line for hours to greet others.

Mary Kay's belief in making everyone feel important extended to company events. If her home could hold the participants of the Seminar winners' reception or other sales force meetings held in Dallas, Mary Kay was willing to host an event for them. Her guests had free run of her house. She even let them look in her closets! If they did, they discovered the spaces were neatly organized, with all Mary Kay's outfits organized by color. Mary Kay kept matching handbags on the shelf above her red suits and dresses, and underneath those she stowed her red shoes. She stored coordinating accessories close by. Not only could guests see where she kept her shoes, they could also try them on! Many women across the United States literally "walked in Mary Kay's shoes."

There were many other ways in which Mary Kay made people feel special. Maria Alvarez from Puerto Rico was the first Latina National Sales Director at Mary Kay Inc.[8] Mary Kay had always admired the beautiful gowns Maria wore at the annual Seminars. When Mary Kay traveled to Puerto Rico to honor Maria as a top Sales Director, Maria insisted that Mary Kay visit her dress designer, who created a stunning red gown and cape that Maria and her designer presented as a gift to Mary Kay.

Mary Kay was grateful, but when she returned home, she discovered that the sequins on the dress made the garment so heavy that she could not walk in it. She knew Maria would be disappointed if she didn't wear the dress. What was Mary Kay's solution? She had a photo shoot wearing the gown and used one of those pictures for the cover of *Applause,* the company's magazine!

When Nancy Thomason speaks about Mary Kay's insistence on making every person feel important, she shares stories from her travels as the head of Mary Kay's security detail. Whenever Mary Kay visited a city, the company would hire a local driving service. If the chauffeur took them to a restaurant, Mary Kay always invited the driver to join her for dinner. Every chauffeur told her that they had never been asked by a client to share a meal. Before departing a city, Mary Kay would write the drivers thank you notes and often give them a copy of her autobiography. She also wrote thank you notes to the hotel personnel and others who had helped her during her visit. Mary Kay was faithful about showing appreciation to everyone who touched her life.

One of Nancy's most poignant memories concerns a homeless person in California. "Mary Kay's limousine was waiting," she recalls. "She was elegantly dressed in a floor-length gown, on her way to accept a prestigious award. As we were leaving the hotel, a homeless woman paused momentarily near the front entrance. Of course, Mary Kay noticed and greeted her warmly. The woman then told Mary Kay she needed a ride across town."

To Nancy's dismay, Mary Kay asked if they could provide the woman with transportation. "I am sure Mary Kay could see the concerned look on my face because of the increased security risk and the possibility of not arriving on time." As they entered the limousine, Mary Kay reached out and patted Nancy's hand, assuring her, "Everything will be fine." And it was. Their guest's destination was near the location of the awards presentation, so they weren't late. As the woman exited the limousine, she expressed her heartfelt appreciation to Mary Kay.

SET GOALS.

A major theme in Mary Kay's speeches was the importance of setting goals. Mary Kay didn't just tell the sales force to set goals; she explained the importance of this habit and how to get it done. Daily goal setting fosters excitement because one arises with an anticipation of achievement and purpose. Mary Kay had a four-step goal-setting program:

1. Decide what you want.
2. Write your goals down.
3. Develop a plan.
4. Set your plan in motion.

In Mary Kay's experience, one important key to goal setting was to write down one's goal. For a goal to be valid, it must be specific, clear, and attainable. Another crucial aspect of goal setting was to put a time limit on a goal. Finally, Mary Kay always suggested sharing the goal with someone else because it holds one accountable and makes the goal more real.

Mary Kay and her son Richard would always set goals for the future of the company. When Mary Kay talked to prospective Beauty Consultants, she would ask them if they could commit to holding five beauty shows each week.[9] If a woman said she didn't think she could make that commitment, Mary Kay would respond, "Then perhaps this career is not for you." The pioneers of her company faithfully held those five shows because they knew Mary Kay expected it of them. Their efforts not only gave them a firm foundation for their own Mary Kay businesses, but were also the underpinning on which Mary Kay Inc. was built.

If a Beauty Consultant was new to the company and did not have any goals, Mary Kay would set one for her. Countless times, the top salespeople in Mary Kay would say that, as a new Beauty Consultant,

Mary Kay told them that they looked like a Sales Director. "That is your goal, isn't it?" she would ask them, nodding her head up and down so that they would nod theirs, too. Later, when those women would tell their success stories, they would relate that—at the time— they didn't even know what a Sales Director did. They had to go home and look up the definition in the Beauty Consultant's manual. Because they had made a commitment to Mary Kay, though, and knew that she believed in them, they did not want to disappoint her and worked hard to reach these goals. These Beauty Consultants were determined to progress in their careers as Mary Kay's encouragement and belief in them continued on each upward step of the Mary Kay ladder of success.

Mary Kay even set goals for tenured Sales Directors. Executive National Sales Director Emeritus Cheryl Warfield once received a phone call from Mary Kay about debuting as a National Sales Director.[10] "Cheryl, we have noticed that you have sixteen first-line directors, five directors-in-qualification, and twenty-four second lines." Richard, who was also on the line, added, "Yes, we can see that you have the numbers to take this step." Cheryl started arguing with Mary Kay, telling her that she wasn't ready. She enjoyed her success as a Sales Director and wanted to be in the top ten position again. "Cheryl," Mary Kay said, "You will be debuting as a National Sales Director onstage this year at Seminar. We are proud of what you have been doing." Cheryl ended up stepping into the position and realized it had been the right move.

When the company first began, the sales force was concentrated in the Dallas area and grew to surrounding states. Another goal of the company was nationwide expansion. To accomplish this, Mary Kay and Richard held a "Break A State" contest, giving recognition to those who were the first to have a new team member in a state where Mary Kay Inc. was not yet established.

Elite Executive National Sales Director Emeritus Anne Newbury recalls the time she went to Dallas for Sales Director training.[11] "There were nine of us in the class. When the week was over, Mary Kay called me into her office. She had a big paper map of the United States with little pinheads on it and told me every time another Sales Director graduated, she put a pinhead on the map. She pointed to a pinhead in Massachusetts and told me that that pin was me. I noticed that there were no other pinheads close to that one. All activity had been in the Southwest in the first six years." Anne took that challenge and ultimately helped the company grow in the Northeast and later into Canada.

One of Mary Kay's frequent admonitions was, "Plan your work and work your plan." To illustrate this third step in goal setting, Mary Kay would share the story of a time when she was hooking a rug. She worked on it whenever she could. Months went by, and she thought she would never finish the project, so she decided to use her goal-setting techniques on the rug. She figured out exactly how much work she could expect to put in each day, created a timetable, and set a deadline. Once she had planned her work, then she "worked her plan," and she finished the rug in about one-third of the time she had already spent haphazardly working on it.

PERSEVERE DESPITE OBSTACLES.

Mary Kay stressed the importance of overcoming obstacles and perseverance during difficult times. She would encourage others to "find a way or make a way." Another motto she often used was: "We fail forward to success." She told people that, if they were ever to compare knees, hers would be the bloodiest, because she had fallen, gotten up, and started all over again so many times. There wasn't a single obstacle women in the company encountered that Mary Kay hadn't personally experienced: abandonment by a husband and divorce, single motherhood, serious illness, the death of a husband and a child, and career disappointments and obstacles. She had gone through it all. No matter what happened, though, she refused to give in or give up. Because of these experiences, Mary Kay related to women and they related to her. Her ability to work through obstacles inspired others to do the same.

Nan Stroud's daughter Kathy had considerable educational challenges, and several school officials advised Nan to remove Kathy from school. When Nan confided her problem to Mary Kay, she insisted that Nan keep looking for answers. After following this advice, the school psychologist found a test that helped identify the right school for Kathy. Today Kathy is thriving, and Nan credits Mary Kay with convincing her to keep advocating for her daughter.

At times, Mary Kay's perseverance bordered on stubbornness. When the company moved from "the gold building" and into a new headquarters, the husband of a Mary Kay employee captured a picture of a rainbow over the roof of the building from which the company was moving. Mary Kay believed that the company had, indeed, been the pot of gold at the end of the rainbow for those who had found success, personal growth, and fulfillment in their Mary Kay careers, so she incorporated that picture into her Seminar speech and asked that the photo be printed on postcards to be sold at Seminar, with the proceeds donated to cancer research.

However, some staff members felt the picture was not professional enough to be used at Seminar, so they didn't print it. When Mary Kay found out, she was undaunted. She continued right on with her speech as she had written it, telling the attendees about the postcard that they could purchase. That evening, the printers worked overtime on the rainbow postcards, which were a big success.

MAINTAIN A POSITIVE ATTITUDE.

Mary Kay believed in the importance of positive thinking, because a negative attitude never accomplished anything. Like all of us, Mary Kay had days when she didn't feel like maintaining a positive, enthusiastic attitude and days when she was frustrated. But she was a role model, and she acted accordingly. She knew that her attitude influenced others, and she stayed positive.

Mary Kay recognized the value of focusing on the positives in one's personal life as well as planting positive seeds in the lives of others. She told us that we should be encouragers, helping others to discover their gifts and develop them. Mary Kay often said that people can achieve much more than they ever dream possible when they know that someone believes in them. As a Christian, she knew that she was called to uplift others, not tear them down.

Being positive was always a big part of the Mary Kay culture. All new employees were advised by coworkers, "If you meet Mary Kay in the elevator and she asks you how you are doing, be sure to say 'Great.'" Not programmed like company veterans, though, the newbies would always be embarrassed because, when they finally met Mary Kay in person, she would ask them the inevitable question. "I'm fine," they would mumble in awe. "No, you are *great!*" Mary Kay would insist. Of course, they couldn't wait to see their coworkers and share how they had blown their elevator meeting with Mary Kay. Soon, though, they would cheerfully be telling her, "Mary Kay, I am great!"

I saw firsthand the impact of positivity on people who joined Mary Kay Inc. as sales force members or staff. If someone had a pessimistic attitude and it didn't change, they couldn't stand the company culture and would leave. Over the years, many employees have shared with me that they couldn't believe how happy everyone was when they came to work for Mary Kay Inc.; they thought it was all fake. They were waiting for "the other shoe to drop," and when it didn't, they noticed that their own attitudes began to change. They discovered that if they looked at each day with what Mary Kay called "positive expectancy," the day went so much more smoothly.

As Mary Kay stated, "I firmly believe that the happiest people are not the ones with the most money, but the ones who really enjoy their work . . . I realized that the real thrill was in being able to do the work I loved . . . I've often said that I enjoy what I do so much that I would work for nothing!"[12]

PEOPLE WILL SUPPORT THAT
WHICH THEY HELP TO CREATE.

Mary Kay often told the staff, "Nothing wilts faster than a laurel rested upon." For a cosmetic company to be successful, it must stay abreast of new technologies, new ingredients, and the latest fashion trends. Over the years, the Mary Kay Inc. product line was constantly updated. Some would fight these changes, but the new products always improved the existing product line.

Because Mary Kay knew how resistant some people can be to change, she had another saying: "People will support that which they help to create." Involving people in the decision-making process was an important tool Mary Kay used in people management. She also wanted to be consulted. At one National Sales Directors meeting, a major change to the skin care line was introduced, and Mary Kay was visibly upset because the Product Development and Marketing staff hadn't shared these new products with her before introducing them to the National Sales Directors. How was Mary Kay supposed to sell them to others when she had not tried them herself? Instead of getting behind the launch, Mary Kay sat there and fumed. When the staff realized what had happened, they immediately apologized and brought her up to date on their research, findings, and launch plans.

Unfortunately, the damage had been done, and she never gave these products her full backing.

On another occasion, the executive floor of the "gold building"—where the company was once headquartered—was updated. The designer brought in painting after painting for Mary Kay to approve for her offices, but she rejected them all, prompting the designer to complain to me, "The trouble is that Mary Kay does not like art." I then replied, "The trouble is that no one has asked Mary Kay what kind of art she likes."

The decorator then set up an appointment for Mary Kay to meet the art broker, who came out of Mary Kay's office after their meeting with a big smile. He confided to me, "Now I know what she wants." A few weeks later, eight paintings of women, children, and landscapes in pastel colors arrived for Mary Kay's inspection. She fell in love when she saw them and ordered every single one.

As a result of Mary Kay's belief that being part of the creation helps with buy-in, one of the company policies has been to always introduce new products, systems, and procedures to the National Sales Directors and then to the Sales Directors before rolling them out to the entire sales force. The company has learned the importance of obtaining the support from the sales force before introducing new products. The sales force must first be sold on any change to be able to enthusiastically present it to their customers.

In the late 1980s, Mary Kay became concerned with ensuring that her principles remained intact after she was no longer with the company. She began writing articles every week for the Sales Directors' publication, as she wanted to leave behind her feelings on topics that she felt were important to the company. She also made a series of cassette tapes, called *Pearls of Wisdom*, sharing the history of the company and the philosophy behind many of the company's policies.

5

MARY KAY THE LEADER

Whoever pursues righteousness and kindness
will find life, righteousness, and honor.

PROVERBS 21:21

Yes, we keep our eye on the bottom line, but it's not an
overriding obsession. To me, P and L doesn't only mean profit
and loss—it also means people and love.

MARY KAY ASH[1]

Mary Kay did not believe in the old saying that leaders are born and not made. She always said that the art of leading could be taught and mastered. She took Dale Carnegie Professional Development courses several times, and she continually read business books and listened to tapes to hone her own leadership skills.

Mary Kay insisted that everyone who joins the Mary Kay independent sales force starts as a Mary Kay Beauty Consultant. Many times, sales managers from other companies would want to come into Mary Kay Inc. at the Sales Director level. However, Mary Kay required everyone—whether they were experienced in sales or not—to learn the business from the ground up. She knew this structure was critical for the company's marketing plan. As she often said, "You cannot teach what you do not know; you cannot lead where you do not go."

When faced with a challenging situation, sales force members and staff members would often ask, "What would Mary Kay do?" This placed an awesome responsibility on Mary Kay's shoulders to set an example! Those who held positions of authority and influence in the company looked to Mary Kay for a pattern of leadership, analyzing what they thought she would do in tough situations.

Mary Kay focused on developing not only her own leadership skills but on helping others become effective as she breathed belief into them. In a 1995 speech to the sales leaders, she said:

> We need leaders who add value to the people and the organization they lead; who work for the benefit of others and not just for their own personal gain; who inspire and motivate rather than intimidate and manipulate; who live with people to know their problems and live with God in order to solve them; and who follow a moral compass that points in the right direction regardless of the trends.[2]

When I was on staff, part of the growth strategy for Mary Kay Inc. leaders was to incorporate forty hours of leadership development in our schedules each year. One could attend company-sponsored classes, read motivational books, or listen to messages on leadership. Since I lived about forty-five minutes from the Mary Kay Inc. building, I listened to a series of leadership-focused CDs by John Maxwell every year. One of his CDs, *Why the Best Leaders Are the Best Leaders,* discusses the specific qualities he found in great leaders, and I was impressed that Mary Kay excelled at every quality he mentioned.

GROWING

Mary Kay said, "I believe that successful people in every field subscribe to a lifetime self-improvement program." In addition to listening to motivational tapes on her way to and from work, Mary Kay also read motivational books. Her formula for reading a self-help book was to read it through once, cover to cover, and then go back and read a chapter a week, putting into practice what it taught.

Mary Kay believed in learning not only from other experts, but also from the sales force. She wanted them to tell her about the successful ideas that they put into practice, and then she would pass them on. At Seminar, she took notes when the top Sales Directors and National Sales Directors gave speeches—and she would share these ideas with those who could not attend Seminar, be it through the company newsletters, her own speeches, or in one-on-one discussions.

Kendra Crist Cross recalls how Mary Kay taught her the importance of never missing an opportunity to learn. At her first Seminar, Kendra was enamored by the opening, but decided she didn't need to attend the classes on the basics of the business. She went back to the hotel and headed for the swimming pool. Keeping an eye on the clock, she planned to be back in her room before her roommate arrived and discovered Kendra in her swimsuit. After Kendra slipped into the elevator, it didn't stop at her floor; instead, it continued upward. When the doors opened, there stood Mary Kay. As Kendra related, "She stepped in and looked me in the eye. I took her hand, shaking it so hard that her head bobbed, and then introduced myself as Kendra Crist Cross. Mary Kay replied, 'Kendra Crist Cross, my guess is that you will never miss another class.'"

Eighteen months later, Kendra attended her first Sales Director orientation. When she stepped up to greet Mary Kay, she again introduced herself. "I know," Mary Kay replied, "You are my elevator girl." Ten years later, on a Top Director trip to Rome, Kendra noticed a vacant seat next to Mary Kay at a grape-stomping event. Kendra asked to join her, and Mary Kay patted the seat. As she told Mary Kay her name, Mary Kay looked at her with a smile and said, "I know. You are my elevator girl."

SERVING OTHERS

Serving others is one of the primary reasons Mary Kay started her company. "The most important justification for being in business is service to others," she insisted.[3] Mary Kay wanted to start a company where women would have the chance to achieve. She had experienced frustration in her own career by not having the opportunity to climb the ladder of success, and she wanted to provide for women what she had been denied. What thrilled Mary Kay the most was hearing success stories from the sales force of how their Mary Kay businesses had helped them afford braces for their children or helped to put them through college. These personal stories from Mary Kay Beauty Consultants made it all worthwhile for Mary Kay.

When she learned that someone in the company had been diagnosed with cancer, she did what she could to show compassion and help them. She made calls, recommended doctors, and, if that Beauty Consultant was in the Dallas area, she would make visits to the hospital to see them.

When Julie Hice, one of Mary Kay's support staff members, was diagnosed with breast cancer, the concern Mary Kay showed for her touched us all. As Julie tells the story: "I'll never forget January 1992. I discovered a lump in one of my breasts. A biopsy soon revealed it to be malignant. At the age of thirty-three, my life changed forever. At that time, I'd worked for Mary Kay Inc. for about ten years. Soon after I learned this news, I got a phone call from Mary Kay. She told me to gather my medical records because she had made an appointment for me with her personal physician, Dr. Amanullah Khan, who, at the time, was the Director of the Mary Kay Ash Center for Cancer Immunotherapy Research at St. Paul Medical Center in Dallas.

"On a very cold Friday morning in January, my husband and I drove through freezing rain to Dr. Khan's office, and, after a long day of tests and meetings, we were surprised to find Mary Kay in Dr. Khan's waiting room. She had come to see how I was doing and encouraged me. She told me I was in the hands of the best oncologist and that everything would be fine. To this day, I'm still touched that she made time to be there for me. She had a million other important things to do, but her first priority was always caring about people. I've been so fortunate in the years since to help carry on her mission by being a channel of hope for others who have been diagnosed with or affected by cancer."

Nancy Thomason also has firsthand experience with Mary Kay's kindness to women in distress. Nancy Thomason and Erma Thomson went on a business trip with Mary Kay. While they were away, Nancy's mother had a cancer scare. Erma believed they should tell Mary Kay about Nancy's mom. Never one to bother Mary Kay with her personal problems, Nancy resisted. Knowing Mary Kay as she did, however, Erma believed Mary Kay would want to know. When she heard the news, Mary Kay insisted on getting Nancy's mother's phone number and called her to put her at ease. Fortunately, Nancy's mother did not have cancer, but Nancy always remembers this kindness.

Anna Ewing, one of the company's early National Sales Directors, recalls a time when she witnessed Mary Kay's servant-hearted qualities in action.[4] Mary Kay encouraged the sharing of ideas, and the company adopted many sales techniques and motivational programs suggested by the sales force.

A sales force member in Minnesota had put together a homemade flip chart of glamour techniques along with the company's marketing plan. Everyone liked the flip chart so much that they began making their own, so Mary Kay Inc. developed a more professional, corporate version. These first flip charts were huge: over twenty-four inches tall. They were to be introduced at a Sales Director workshop. Mary Kay invited everyone who was to teach a class on the new flip chart to her room. After the session, each Sales Director was to carry the new flip chart and all the accompanying products to her class.

Mary Kay's training session took longer than anticipated, and she worried that the women would not get to their classes on time. She inquired where each one was teaching and learned that Anna's class was the farthest away. Mary Kay insisted on carrying not only the flip chart but also all the products for Anna. Anna didn't want Mary Kay to do this and was embarrassed, but Mary Kay insisted because she always wanted to help her Sales Directors, even if it meant literally carrying their burdens. Anna told me that she learned a big lesson that day: to be a leader, you must be a servant.

MODELING

Women pursuing careers today owe much to trailblazers like Mary Kay. In the 1960s, the workplace was not a friendly place for women.[5] When women became pregnant, they were released from their jobs. Women couldn't open a bank account, borrow money, or get a credit card.[6] In 1963, women made about fifty-nine cents to every dollar that men made.[7] But Mary Kay knew a woman's brain was worth more than fifty cents on the dollar.

Although Mary Kay believed that women needed equal pay, access to professional jobs, and freedom from sexual harassment, she didn't think women should burn their bras or dress and talk like men. She believed that God had given women special qualities. She was proud to be a woman and to "think like a woman."

In a time when women did not lead corporations, Mary Kay made the decision to start her own company and became a role model for others. Mary Kay's desire was that women be paid commensurate to their abilities, so she developed a marketing plan with an open-ended ladder of success. She gave women financial opportunity through Mary Kay Inc. Many of the company's top saleswomen have become millionaires, and those who join this "Millionaires Club" are celebrated at Seminar each year.

Mary Kay truly practiced what she preached, and she modeled leadership to the sales force and to those of us on staff. She lived her example in both her personal and business life. To her, the two were inseparable. As her renown grew, Mary Kay realized that each of her actions and words was "in the spotlight." She often expressed to me that she never wanted to disappoint people, and she always strived to live up to what was expected of her as a leader.

In her book, *In Pink*, Doretha Dingler recalls a Top Ten Sales Director trip with Mary Kay in 1985, on which the group saw Mary Kay model bravery. The Sales Directors, staff, and Mary Kay were cruising the Mediterranean Sea aboard the *Stella Solaris* when the passengers were called to a meeting. They were told that the *Achille Lauro*, a ship in nearby waters, had been hijacked on its way from Alexandria, Egypt, to Port Said, Egypt. The Sales Directors were naturally frightened when they learned that the ship's 438 passengers had been taken captive by the hijackers and that one wheelchair-bound passenger had been mercilessly murdered. The women decided among themselves that they did not want to proceed with the cruise. As they were talking, Mary Kay appeared. She told them that arrangements were being made to transport them to Athens, Greece, if they wanted to go, but that she would stay on the ship with anyone who wished to remain. Of course, if Mary Kay stayed, the Sales Directors decided that they could continue the trip. The captain assured them that they were being diverted to Egypt where they would be safe. They pulled into port and docked in the middle of the night, and the next morning they discovered that they were next to the *Achille Lauro*. As a group, the Sales Directors were wholeheartedly impressed with Mary Kay's calmness and her willingness to stay with those who wanted to continue the trip they'd worked so hard to earn.

One of Mary Kay's biggest challenges in setting an example came in 1975. A group of Mary Kay executives thought it would be a great idea for Mary Kay to hold a ten-show week—she could set the pace for the sales force. Holding a beauty show meant booking the appointments, presenting the products, taking the orders, booking upcoming appointments, and talking about the Mary Kay opportunity. The sales department theorized that if Mary Kay, the Chairman of the Board, could tackle a ten-show week along with her busy schedule, no one else could have an excuse. Mary Kay had not held a skin care class, then called a "beauty show," in fifteen years, so she was quite reluctant and nervous. However, she recognized that the staff was right: this would prove that the ten-show week goal was realistic, and she would lead the way. The company then organized and promoted a national ten-show week campaign.

Mary Kay ordered a showcase and went through training just like any new Beauty Consultant. LaQueta McCollum remembers walking into the Mary Kay headquarters and meeting Mary Kay, who told her, "I have been trying to call you. You have got to train me." LaQueta was flabbergasted. Mary Kay then explained, "Our sales department wants me to hold a ten-show week. I haven't held a show in fifteen years. I will be at your meeting on Monday morning."

At that time, LaQueta held her meetings at the Mary Kay headquarters, and on Monday morning, Mary Kay sat on the front row with her notebook and tape recorder. After the meeting, she called LaQueta to her office, complimented LaQueta on her presentation, and then asked, "Now, will you help me fill out an order? I haven't done that in years, either." It was so busy in the office that day, however, that Mary Kay asked LaQueta to come to her home the next day. LaQueta took her youngest daughter, Tracy, and Mary Kay served them cookies and lemonade. Mary Kay then asked LaQueta to be her assistant for the week. That week turned into one of the busiest in LaQueta's career; she helped Mary Kay with her ten shows in the early parts of the day and then held her own ten-show week in the late afternoons and evenings.

GPS was unheard of in 1975, so LaQueta would meet at Mary Kay's house and follow her to the location of the show. Mary Kay would come to a stop sign, do a quick look, and then zoom through the intersection. She never completely stopped. LaQueta told her afterwards, "Mary Kay, you are the hot-roddingest grandmother I have ever had to follow!"

Mary Kay practiced diligently for her ten-show week, reading the training manuals and all accompanying literature. She asked her hostesses not to share with the guests that she would be conducting the shows, but few attendees recognized her (this event was in 1975, when the company was still young and Mary Kay was not well-known). Mary Kay related that she received the same excuses from potential customers that she had always heard, such as, "I just bought new make-up," or "I don't have the money right now." Always a master saleswoman, Mary Kay put into practice what she taught.

When her ten-show week was over, Mary Kay was flying high with excitement because she had made more money that week holding skin care classes than she did as Chairman of the Board! But what thrilled her even more was the delight that came from helping women with their self-image. The excitement and joy Mary Kay received from this experience was a wonderful gift to her, and she talked about it for years to come.

LISTENING

Mary Kay built her company by listening to and welcoming suggestions from those below her. When the company was young, all Sales Directors would come to Dallas once a month for meetings. They were encouraged to bring their ideas and share them. Mary Kay would tell them, "If I have an idea and you have an idea, we each have one, but when we share our ideas, we each have two." After these meetings, Mary Kay would send memos to any absent Sales Directors, highlighting these new ideas.

Promptly answering correspondence and phone calls was another form of listening that Mary Kay practiced. She strongly felt that if someone took the time to write or call, what they had to say was important and should be acknowledged as quickly as possible. For this reason, she had a staff of ten people to keep up with all her correspondence, calls, appointments, newsletters, and the many projects she would initiate.

However, the most important listening skill that Mary Kay taught everyone was to focus your attention on the person to whom you are talking. She would always look directly at those speaking and never take her attention away from them until they had finished. She would stand in line for hours to greet sales force members, and she always gave the last person in line the same personal attention that she gave the first.

When someone came to Mary Kay for advice, she would ask, "What do you think you should do?" Then she would listen. Mary Kay said that if one listens long enough, the speaker will come up with the solution.

Everyone who visited Mary Kay's office noticed her horseshoe-shaped couch. When groups came to see her, she moved her chair from behind her desk and placed it in front of the couch so that she formed a circle. She would then speak to each person individually, asking questions and always listening. Every month, she invited to her office any employees celebrating their ten-year anniversaries and have each one of them tell her not only about what they did at Mary Kay Inc., but also about their families. She always had time, no matter her other commitments, to hear what was important in the lives of everyone in the company.

In the late 1980s, Mary Kay Inc. instituted a generous retirement program for its National Sales Directors. One of the requirements of the program was mandatory retirement for National Sales Directors aged sixty-five; the retiree would then become a National Sales Director Emeritus. The first women who had to retire under this program were devastated; they didn't want their Mary Kay careers to end. Many on the Mary Kay Inc. staff, though, could not understand the National Sales Directors' anguish since the retirement plan was generous and was certainly to their benefit. But these were the pioneer women who had helped Mary Kay build her dream company, and they loved their roles of encouraging and helping women.

Mary Kay understood how they felt. Based on what she heard, she sensed that the women felt rejected, so she wanted to do something for them. She invited them to an emeriti-only reunion. There was only one requirement: everyone had to bring one clean joke. After telling their jokes, the women continued to reminiscence on the funny things that had happened to each of them as they had built their businesses and on the good times they had shared with Mary Kay. Her plan was a success. Mary Kay had heard their comments of unhappiness and determined to make them feel important to her and to the company.

OBSERVING

In addition to listening, the best leaders observe what goes on around them. They will not isolate themselves but instead interact with their people. They want to witness firsthand what happens within the ranks.

When Mary Kay Inc. was smaller, Mary Kay would sit in the audience during meetings and observe. When she saw someone who was obviously upset, she would call a staff member to her side and say, "I think there may be a problem. Could you go and check on her?"

Sue Kirkpatrick had such an experience. At one conference she attended, she arrived with a burden on her heart. She wanted to share it with Mary Kay and receive her counsel, but Sue didn't have the courage to mention it. When Sue arrived back at her hotel, Erma Thomson called her on behalf of Mary Kay. "Sue, Mary Kay just had a feeling that there was something else you wanted to talk to her about, and here she is." Sue cried and poured her heart out to Mary Kay. As Sue says, "My problem and her response to me is not nearly as important as the lesson she taught. I remember thinking, 'Lord, help me to be an intuitive leader like Mary Kay.'"

Mary Kay would often look around to see who was interested in what was being taught and who was taking notes. She would then seek those people out and encourage them. One National Sales Director tells of the time Mary Kay came up to her and told her that she had noticed this National Sales Director had been at the same level for several years. "Next time," Mary Kay said, "I want to see you as a Sales Director."

Elite Executive National Sales Director Emeritus Kathy Helou remembers a year when she was onstage as a Top Ten Director.[8] The group also included two very pregnant Sales Directors and one who had just had surgery. Mary Kay looked at them and had three chairs brought onstage immediately, insisting they all sit down. As Kathy told me, "I was touched that she was observing what was right for these women, not what looked right from a logistics point of view."

As the company grew and there was an increased demand for Mary Kay's attention, even top sales force members valued her time. But with her love for people, Mary Kay always wanted to be a part of what was happening.

Cheryl Warfield recalls one time when she held her group meeting in a hospitality room after Seminar, and they entered the room at the same time as Mary Kay. Not wanting to bother her, Cheryl tried to redirect her group elsewhere, but when Mary Kay saw what Cheryl was doing, she personally invited them into the room, kicked off her shoes, and joined them for an informal chat. As the group was leaving, Mary Kay said to Cheryl, "Tell your Wonder Women I think they are wonderful." Before that chance meeting, Cheryl had called her national area the "Warfield Winners." Because of Mary Kay's words, they then became the "Wonder Women."

Mary Kay would even notice what others wore, especially jewelry, and would ask to borrow pieces for an occasion if they complemented one of her outfits. She always returned the item promptly—with a thank you note. Mary Kay also lent her own items. After her stroke, one of her caregivers, Angel Morrison Holley, was getting married. Mary Kay lent Angel her canary diamond necklace to wear on her wedding day. Although Mary Kay couldn't go to the wedding, she wanted to do something special for Angel—and that necklace enabled her to be present at the wedding in the form of Angel's "something borrowed."

RELATING TO OTHERS

In talking about vision, John Maxwell said that great leaders see farther and broader and bigger than their people, but they also can see through their people's eyes. This was certainly true of Mary Kay. Whenever a policy or procedure changed, Mary Kay would always consider the impact of that change through the eyes of those it affected.

Mary Kay could relate to a new Beauty Consultant on a limited budget who chose to invest in her career even though she didn't have extra money. She knew the frustration of making a presentation with no sales. She never forgot where she came from and the struggles that she faced as a single mother.

Mary Kay constantly reminded the staff that the company's customers were their sales force members—the sales force were the ones purchasing products directly from the company—and that most of them pursue their Mary Kay careers to help put bread on the table for their families. If they could not make money, then they would move on to something else. She related to the sales force because direct sales was her background, and she loved helping women. Mary Kay knew what women wanted. When she had made it to the boardroom in a previous company, her ideas were dismissed: "Mary Kay, you're thinking like a woman." She believed that thinking like a woman was a good thing, and she never stopped doing so. When she thought like a woman, she had a great influence on women.[9]

To relate to others, one must be open with others. Mary Kay would talk to anybody about what was bothering her. If the maintenance man came into her office to adjust the temperature and something was on Mary Kay's mind, she chatted with him about it. This is what people loved about Mary Kay: she shared with all of us what was going on in her life, whether individually or onstage in front of a huge assembly. She felt she could relate to anyone and reveal her own concerns.

As a Top Sales Director, Sue Kirkpatrick often had the opportunity to come to Dallas to teach new Sales Directors, and Mary Kay always invited her into her office. During one of those meetings, Mary Kay shared what was on her heart. "It was almost as if she was thinking out loud, and I happened to be the one listening." Mary Kay said to

Sue, "There are three major things that cause women stress—money, health, and relationships. Strong women can handle one at a time, but it takes an exceptionally strong woman to handle more than one, so we need to take care of those three things and do what we can to manage them."

Mary Kay believed in developing relationships, and she wanted to personally get to know the people around her. Sue lived in a small town in Indiana with a population of seventeen thousand, called New Castle. The nearest large city was Indianapolis. Mary Kay visited New Castle twice to honor Sue for building a top unit, but in her small town, the only lodging for travelers was a motel. When Erma Thomson called Sue to make accommodations for Mary Kay and Mel, Sue suggested the couple stay at a nice hotel in Indianapolis and be transported back and forth. Erma reiterated, "Mary Kay wants to stay where you live."

Sue then booked the little motel's best room, the bridal suite. The only difference between it and every other room in the facility was that it had flocked wallpaper, shag carpet, a velour bedspread, and a mirror on the ceiling. Mary Kay and Mel were very gracious and humble about the arrangements, because relating to Sue by staying in her hometown was more important for Mary Kay than staying in a fancy hotel.

In late 1979, Mel was diagnosed with lung cancer. A Mary Kay Leadership Conference was scheduled for January 1980, but Mary Kay did not plan to go; she would not leave Mel's side. Nine days before this conference, Mel passed away. Mary Kay was devastated. At the last minute, she made the decision to attend the Leadership Conference. Many of the Sales Directors in attendance knew Mel personally. Mary Kay went and openly shared her grief while being with people she loved and who loved both her and Mel. It was a touching meeting, and everyone who attended never forgot her heartfelt grief.

In 1991, Mary Kay's daughter Marylyn passed away. Because of Mary Kay's passion for helping find a cure for cancer through research, many people assumed that Marylyn had died from cancer, but the real cause of her death was pneumonia. Marylyn had a case of what she called "the crud," but she felt good enough to go grocery shopping. When Marylyn returned home, she did not feel well and she told her husband that she needed to lie down. A short time later, she asked him to call an ambulance. Marylyn passed away before the ambulance arrived. Mary Kay was devastated and discovered the truth of the saying that children should never go before their parents. However, this devastating event inspired a new mission for Mary Kay: whenever anyone had a lingering cold or cough, she would fervently urge them to see a doctor as soon as possible because of what happened to Marylyn.

Nancy Thomason recalls a time when she drove Mary Kay home in the early 1990s. Mary Kay began relating a phone call she had received that day about a Beauty Consultant who had been diagnosed with cancer. As Mary Kay related the details of the call, Nancy could hear her getting emotional. She looked over and saw a tear run down Mary Kay's cheek. Nancy couldn't help but think that, in all the years she had worked for Mary Kay, and with all the tragedy the woman had experienced, Mary Kay had never lost her compassion.

DEVELOPING PEOPLE

Mary Kay wrote a book in 1984 on developing people titled *Mary Kay on People Management*.[10] She was an expert in this leadership quality.

Mary Kay had the wonderful ability to see the potential in people and make them feel important. If she needed information from someone within our company, she would ask me to obtain that person's direct number. She would then call them, saying, "I have a problem. Can you help me?"

Another way that Mary Kay developed people was through encouraging them to dream and to set goals. She believed in applauding accomplishment, but once a goal was reached, she was always urging that person to strive for the next level of success. For many years, she personally presented all the awards at Seminar. After congratulating a winner, she would encourage her to strive for the next level. She would tell a runner-up, "Next year, you are going to be Queen," or she'd tell a Sales Director whose unit had reached $850,000 in yearly production, "Now it's time you did the million."

Arlene Lenarz was the number one National at Mary Kay Inc. for seven years before her retirement. Before she joined Mary Kay Inc., Arlene had resigned from her nursing position to care for her four small children. When thinking about her children's college educations, however, she realized that she needed some way to earn money. Arlene's sister, who was a Beauty Consultant, introduced her to the opportunities found through Mary Kay Inc., and Arlene joined the company in 1972. At that time, Arlene was shy and lacking in self-confidence. She discovered that Mary Kay had mapped out a well-defined ladder of success for her to follow and provided the training and educational materials needed to build a successful business. "Mary Kay gave us a railroad track to run on," Arlene recalls. "She set a strategy of success before us. She gave us the vehicle; we supplied the steam." As Arlene was challenged to reach new levels, she discovered that her self-confidence grew.

When it came to Mary Kay's philosophy on the bottom-line value of the people in her company, others often misquote her by insisting, "Mary Kay said that P&L means people and love, not profit and loss."

What Mary Kay really said was, "P&L means people and love, *and* profit and loss." Mary Kay was a leader who cared about people and she founded her company to help people. However, she also knew that a company needs to turn a profit to stay in business, especially when the continuation of the company is at stake. Mary Kay recognized that business owners must make tough decisions that also involve people they care about.

Empowering Others

Mary Kay had a sixth sense for finding the right people for a job, giving them that responsibility, and letting them execute the plan. She was never a micromanager. As someone who worked with her closely for twenty-five years, I saw firsthand this leadership quality of empowering others. Mary Kay generated a lot of ideas, but once she handed over a project to me or to others on her support staff, she was confident that we would get it done efficiently, in the Mary Kay Way. She never looked over our shoulders to see what we were doing, she never asked for progress reports, and she never asked how we would accomplish a task: she simply believed in us.

Photographer Barry McCoy began taking pictures for Mary Kay Inc. in 1987, primarily of Mary Kay and the new Sales Directors. The first time he did a photo shoot with Mary Kay, he took an array of proofs to her office so she could select the one she liked. "Which one do you think is best?" she asked him. When Barry pointed out the photo he preferred, Mary Kay replied, "Then why did you show me all the others? You're the professional."

One of the greatest examples of Mary Kay empowering others was the way that she passed her torch to the National Sales Directors. At every opportunity, she told them that—when she was no longer leading the company—it was up to them to continue sharing the principles and foundations she had established. After she passed away, this responsibility became a serious role for the National Sales Directors. While they had always been exceptional leaders, they felt charged to *be* Mary Kay after her death. The Nationals became hostesses at Mary Kay events and taught in her place. They took on her role of greeting the sales force, and they have literally become Mary Kay to those women. They embody Mary Kay's loving and caring attitude; they look people in the eyes, they encourage, and they inspire. Mary Kay's commission to them was not just empty words. Mary Kay empowered the National Sales Directors to be her, and they have stepped up to this role.

MOTIVATING

When she was alive and running her company, Mary Kay motivated others through her example and enthusiasm. Today, she motivates others through her legacy and the example she left behind. She had a vision, and she knew how to pull others into that vision.

Kathy Helou recalls one of the trips that she was awarded. Kathy accompanied Mary Kay to a castle in Europe for the farewell dinner. The menus were printed on parchment paper with the date and courses for the evening, and attendees started asking Mary Kay to sign their menus. She had a purple pen in her purse, and she signed one menu after another. In the end, she had signed menus for everyone in the room, and she was never able to eat. When the line evaporated, Mary Kay turned to Kathy and said, "Where is your menu?" Kathy told Mary Kay that she didn't need to sign her menu because she had learned so much from watching her interact with people. Mary Kay insisted, and on Kathy's menu she wrote, "I believe that you will be the first Sales Director to break the two-million-dollar barrier. I know you can do it!"

National Sales Director Sherrill Steinman watched this exchange, and she remarked to Kathy afterwards, "I saw what Mary Kay wrote on your paper, and I think you will, too." Kathy framed the menu, hung it on her wall, and sometimes carried it with her to motivate herself and her unit. By the next Seminar, she broke the company record as her unit exceeded two million dollars in retail sales. She told Mary Kay, "Because you planted the seed inside of me, I was able to reach this goal!"

Among the Mary Kay sales force, those who were most impacted by Mary Kay's teachings were the National Sales Directors. Shortly after Mary Kay's death, Sandy Miller, a Senior National Sales Director Emeritus in Indiana, wrote this about the lessons she learned from Mary Kay:

> Dear Mary Kay,
>
> You have mentored so many of us, and did you know that we welcome our responsibility to pass on our heritage here and in every country we open?
>
> How did you know that we could be forever blessed by following the Golden Rule and taking God as our partner?
>
> How did you know that giving really does come back tenfold and that adopting the Go-Give Spirit would set us apart from everyone?
>
> Did you know that we were watching when you were kind to the waitresses, maids, mailmen, and cooks, and that we learned "it's nice to be important, but more important to be nice"?
>
> Did you know that when your husband Mel passed away and you still attended the conference in St. Louis, you taught us strength, commitment, responsibility, and to "put on a happy face"?

Did you know that we were always confident that you would do the right thing and that your confidence gave us security and taught us integrity?

Did you know that, as we watched when you stood in your heels for hours and hours greeting everyone warmly, you taught us tolerance, humility, and patience?

Did you know that we saved all your letters and that your thank you notes taught us to do the same, and taught us the importance of gratitude and appreciation?

Mary Kay, how did you know that, when you stood firm in dressing like a lady while current fashion trends said different, you taught us fashion is fickle and style is always, and that we would one day be identified with class and style?

Mary Kay, did you know that when you were no longer able to be with us physically, we still felt your presence and love and we welcomed the responsibility to carry on your legacy even more?

Did you know that one day you would establish a charitable foundation to fund cancer research inspired with our support, and from this we experienced joy and learned humanitarianism?

Mary Kay, did you know that the business and people skills you taught us would one day be quoted, copied, envied, published, embraced, and admired by many from all walks of life?

Do you have any idea of the multitude of lives that have been touched because of you and your dream? Not only ours, but our children's, and their children's, and the children still to come.

You always said we would make a difference in this old world, and we are. Do you know our hearts beat in sync with yours, that we are proud of our heritage, traditions, and you? We know God is smiling with approval. Thanks for creating big girl dreams.[11]

The Golden Rule Principle

Many leadership experts never mention the Golden Rule principle because it is almost nonexistent in today's corporate world. But Mary Kay's insistence on operating her company on this Christian principle is the primary reason for her astounding success. Years after Mary Kay had grown her company so big, in a grand irony, she received a call from the president of World Gift. He wanted to learn her business secret. When Mary Kay informed him that she had used the same suggestions she'd tried to give him years before, he didn't believe her. He kept asking, "Now, Mary Kay, tell me how you *really* did it.'"

He was not the only one skeptical of the fact that one of the primary reasons for Mary Kay's success came from her operating the company on the Golden Rule. According to Dick Bartlett, Vice Chairman of Mary Kay Inc., "I can recall many an investment banker coming away from a meeting with Mary Kay and whispering to me, 'She doesn't really believe that, does she? You can't run a billion-dollar business that way, can you?' These bankers had no clue as to how wrong they were. The answer to both questions they asked was an emphatic yes."[12]

Over the years, however, there has often been a misconception involving the Golden Rule. When sales force and staff encounter those whose behaviors are questionable or are faced with decisions with which they do not agree, they will say, "Well, those people are not living by the Golden Rule." But they have it all wrong. The Golden Rule concerns one person: you. The implied pronoun—the subject of the sentence—is you. It does not say, "Others should treat me the way

I want to be treated." The Golden Rule states: "*You* do under others as *you* would have others do unto *you*."

The Golden Rule tells us how to treat others; it does not guarantee that others will reciprocate our behavior. In many cases, they probably won't. We can only control our own actions, not the actions of others. As mentioned previously, Mary Kay said she returned good for evil many times; in the end, she knew she did the right thing. She believed that—somehow—everything would work out if she treated others with respect, kindness, and deference—and it did.

6

MARY KAY THE ROCK STAR

For you bless the righteous, O Lord;
you cover him with favor as with a shield.

Psalm 5:12

I consider them to be my daughters; they consider
me to be their mother, and we love each other.

Mary Kay Ash[1]

When I first joined the company in 1971, I was amazed by Mary Kay's charisma. I had learned the definition of the word in high school . . . but here was someone who literally drew people to her for inspiration and whose presence affected people. And to top it all off—she was a great-grandmother! When Sales Directors brought prospective Beauty Consultants to meet Mary Kay, the newbies were literally speechless in her presence. They couldn't even remember their names. After a few minutes, Mary Kay made them feel comfortable and engaged them in conversation.

Mary Kay did not only have this effect upon the sales force; people were drawn to her everywhere she went. On Cheryl Warfield's first National Sales Director trip, the women went shopping in La Jolla, a neighborhood of San Diego, California. Mary Kay was recovering from knee surgery and used a scooter to get around easily. She wanted to visit with everyone, so she zipped to and fro on this scooter, going in and out of the shops, many of which were frequented by various celebrities and the well-to-do. Once inside a shop, Mary Kay interacted with everyone there. Shop owners would even follow her out of their stores and onto the sidewalk. She had a great time, spreading joy wherever she went. Mary Kay became the center of everyone's attention as people noticed her and began smiling.

The National Sales Directors loved seeing the awe on peoples' faces when they encountered Mary Kay, and they loved watching her draw others in with her charisma. They were proud to be associated with her. In the eyes of the sales force, Mary Kay was a rock star. By this, I mean she was a person they admired, and they became emotionally attached to her. She had given them a career that blessed them financially, spiritually, and personally.

The sales force wanted to emulate Mary Kay because she believed that women could climb to whatever heights they desired to achieve their goals, and the earning potential she'd created through the company was lucrative. Mary Kay's business gave housewives the opportunity to get outside the house, yet still have time with their children. Those who took advantage of a Mary Kay career gained so much more than just extra money for the family, though. Mary Kay taught women to be confident, to set goals, to keep their priorities in the proper perspective, to step out of their comfort zones, and to become professional businesswomen. The sales force loved Mary Kay for what she had given them, and their gratitude spilled over with enthusiasm.

When Mary Kay walked into her interview on *The 700 Club* in 1981, sales force members in the audience stood up and sang "Mary Kay Enthusiasm." This was a song that members sang at Mary Kay meetings to the tune of the old camp song, "I've Got that Joy, Joy, Joy." The host of *The 700 Club*, Pat Robertson, was speechless. "Mary Kay," he exclaimed, "How do you get such loyalty?" Mary Kay replied, "I consider them to be my daughters, they consider me to be their mother, and we love each other."[2]

Trying to move Mary Kay through a crowd of Mary Kay Beauty Consultants was like trying to move a Hollywood star through a group of admirers. At special events, such as Seminar and Leadership Conference, before Mary Kay would step into the lobby from an elevator, her staff would check to see if they could easily cross with her to the hotel entrance. Even if no one was there initially, someone would invariably spot Mary Kay from far away and yell, "There's Mary Kay!" In a matter of moments, Mary Kay would be swarmed by the sales force. But she never forgot her commitment to always treat everyone as if there was a sign around the person's neck reading, "Make me feel important." She took pictures with and talked to all who approached her, which often caused her to be late for whichever event she was attending.

To avoid detection, the staff decided to take Mary Kay through hotel kitchens and onto service elevators, just like movie stars and other dignitaries. When most celebrities walk through these unglamorous areas, they ignore the staff—but not Mary Kay. The first time she stepped into a hotel kitchen before a company event, Mary Kay talked to the staff as they worked and asked them, "How are you doing?" When they would say they were fine, she would invariably tell them, "No, you're *great*!"

Every time she stepped into a kitchen, Mary Kay talked to the staff and told them how great they were. By the end of her stay, when she would step into the kitchen, the hotel employees would line up in a receiving line, and she would walk along and shake everyone's hand in greeting. Many times, hotel managers would write to Mary Kay and say, "We don't know what you did for our kitchen staff, but their attitudes have been tremendous since your visit."

When Mary Kay stepped onstage at company events, she was greeted by thunderous applause. At one event, however, sales force enthusiasm was at a higher pitch than normal. Every spring, the company held multiple conferences across the country on the same day. Since Mary Kay could not attend all of these meetings, only one city had the privilege of hosting a live appearance by Mary Kay. The women in other cities would watch a prerecorded message from her. The company would host a contest for one of these cities to earn her appearance. The winning city was announced during the meeting; Mary Kay would step onstage at the winning location and that audience would burst into cheers of enthusiasm.

Nancy Thomason would always warn new staff members about the sales force's reaction, telling them that women would rush the stage and that their job was to protect the teleprompters. Never having seen this type of adoration from the sales force, the newcomers did not believe Nancy. As the attendees charged the stage, Nancy would chuckle as she watched the new staff members clutch the teleprompters in disbelief. These women wanted to get as close to Mary Kay as possible because she would always reach out and shake hands with those within arm's length.

Mary Kay loved motivational books and speakers, especially those who were Christians. She developed a warm friendship with Dr. Robert Schuller, founder of the Crystal Cathedral and author of thirty-seven books; he also spoke at the 1976 Mary Kay Seminar.[3] He had a saying that Mary Kay used in her speeches: "When you come to a mountain, you don't quit. You go over, under, around, or through whatever obstacles stand in your way."

Dr. Schuller invited Mary Kay to speak at the Crystal Cathedral several times, particularly for women's conferences. As always, whenever Mary Kay spoke, people lined up after the event to meet her and shake her hand. After an engagement one Saturday evening, the line to meet Mary Kay was so long that the church staff interrupted the meet and greet, saying they had to get the church ready for the next day's Sunday service. Mary Kay replied, "Well, we'll just move out into the parking lot." The parking lot lights were turned off, so people turned on their car lights. Mary Kay stood there until 12:30 in the morning, greeting every person.

Mary Kay never went into a city without holding an event for the Mary Kay sales force. As part of her last trip to New York City, she spoke at a large gathering before thousands of women. When the event ended, guests were asked to stay in their seats while she departed. In the hopes of whisking Mary Kay away to the airport for her flight back to Dallas, her two hired drivers, hotel security, protective detail, and staff surrounded her to get her to the waiting car. But when Mary Kay stepped into the lobby, she was met by a crowd of sales force members who had not been able to obtain a seat in the ballroom—because it was filled to capacity—and had waited patiently, hoping to get a glimpse of her as she exited.

Mary Kay did not disappoint these waiting women. She waved and smiled at the sales force, but as she was moved through the crowd, someone caught her attention. Out of the corner of her eye, she noticed a woman wearing a Mary Kay pin sitting in a wheelchair. As Nancy Thomason described, "She broke away from the security detail and went to the woman, kneeling down to speak to her at eye level. She took the woman's hand between her two hands, thanked her for coming and spoke to her for a few minutes. A hush settled over all those in the lobby clamoring to see Mary Kay." Despite the rush to get her out of the building and all the hubbub around her, Mary Kay focused on this woman as if she were the only one in the lobby.

Mary Kay's rock star status was not just confined to those among the company. After the *60 Minutes* interview, Mary Kay became a highly visible figure, especially around Dallas. When she went to the grocery store, she would invariably be recognized. People would ask for her autograph, and if paper was unavailable, she would sign whatever was thrust into her hands, including a can of green beans!

This adulation extended to countries around the world. Nancy Thomason once accompanied Mary Kay on a trip to Japan with the top saleswomen. Nancy felt she wouldn't need to worry as much about Mary Kay's protection because she couldn't imagine that the people there would recognize Mary Kay; to her surprise, as they walked the streets, people would stop and stare at Mary Kay. Nancy would then hear them excitedly point and cry, "Mary Kay!"

As Dick Bartlett always told sales force members, "I have known two people that have the atmosphere of good surrounding them. I sat on a plane once next to Martin Luther King, Jr., and he had a glow of goodness all around him. And the second person is Mary Kay. When she walks onstage, the whole room feels her goodness. It radiates from her. It spreads throughout the room."

7

MARY KAY THE PHILANTHROPIST

Whoever is generous to the poor lends to the LORD,
and he will repay him for his deed.

PROVERBS 19:17

It is important to remember that you do not have
to change a certain number of lives. By reaching out to
just one person, you can make a difference. That person can
be anyone—a child, a friend, a customer, a homeless person,
anyone at all . . . You don't have to win the Nobel Peace Prize
. . . Making a difference requires only your willingness to
give to others—the more often the better.

MARY KAY ASH[1]

Mary Kay always tithed, giving generously to her church and other causes in which she believed. As she became a public figure, donation requests poured into her office, and she took time to personally consider each of them. If a cause touched her heart, Mary Kay had one of her staff members investigate the organization to ensure it properly used its donation monies. She was particularly interested in the percentage of donations that went to the cause and the percentage that went to the administration. If Mary Kay felt that the organization did not use funds wisely, she would not give.

She was committed to being a good steward of all God entrusted to her.

One of Mary Kay's favorite examples of God's faithfulness involves the time she was asked by her pastor to speak to their congregation about the need for a new children's building. When she was a young mother, she taught Primers Sunday School, so children's programs had always interested her. Mary Kay accepted the invitation, knowing she had six weeks to prepare her plea. During that time, she thought about what she might say, but nothing came to her.

The morning she was to speak, Mary Kay's alarm didn't go off, so she was running late. To make matters worse, she hadn't written one word of her speech. So she asked God to help her. "You'll have to tell me what to say, Lord," she recalls praying. When relating this story to me, she said, "And then I stopped dead in the middle of putting on my makeup, because a thought had come to me so clearly and suddenly that I was shocked." She heard the Lord telling her that, after her speech, she should offer to match the amount of donations given that day.

After telling stories about her time as a young children's Sunday School teacher and how strongly she felt about teaching them Biblical lessons, Mary Kay announced that she would match any funds raised. Returning to her seat, she noticed that the congregation remained rather silent, and she wondered if her plea had had any effect. At the end of the service, the pastor told the congregation that they had until five o'clock that evening for their donations to qualify for Mary Kay's matching fund. When that hour came, Mary Kay waited anxiously for his phone call, but it wasn't until the next morning that the Chairman of the Building Committee contacted her.

Before he told her what they had raised, the Chairman gave Mary Kay the opportunity to back out of her commitment. Mary Kay was adamant that she would keep her promise. When he told her that they had raised over $100,000, she was astonished. Since the congregation had to give cash for their pledge, she believed that she should, too.

After the call ended, Mary Kay sat at her desk wondering how she could raise the money. Then the phone rang. Her son Richard was calling with news that the oil wells in which she had invested were gushers, and her share that month would be over $100,000. Mary Kay was so grateful to God, and she shared this testimony of her belief and God's faithfulness frequently. I often heard her say, "You can't out-give God."

At Mary Kay Inc.'s Thirtieth Anniversary Seminar, the staff created a segment for Mary Kay on the program agenda titled "This Is Your Life." People from her past said a few words about their relationship and then came onstage to congratulate her. She was delighted with this presentation because she was reunited with so many lifetime friends.

The story from Reverend and Mrs. Moses Reagan surprised me the most, as I had never heard their story. As they related, back in the late 1960s, Mary Kay had read about their Tabernacle Baptist Church collecting S&H Green Stamps to purchase a van for transporting their children's ministry. Mary Kay had recently been to an S&H store and couldn't find anything she wanted or needed, so she decided to donate her Green Stamps to the church. She left for her own church early one Sunday morning so she could stop by Tabernacle Baptist first. She soon found herself in a poorer section of town and had difficulty finding the church, which turned out to be a small building.

Once inside the church, Mary Kay approached a woman and asked for Reverend Moses Reagan. The woman told her that he was not available, but that she was his wife, and she was very thankful for the Green Stamps. As they conversed, Mrs. Reagan received a phone call from the beginners' Sunday School teacher: she had fallen ill and would not be able to teach her class that morning. When Mrs. Reagan expressed her distress at not having anyone available to cover the class, Mary Kay told her that she had taught beginners' Sunday School for many years and would be happy to fill in. The Tabernacle Baptist Church was an African American church, and Mary Kay wore a white outfit that day. The Reagans related in their "This Is Your Life" presentation that the children at the church couldn't stop staring at her, calling her their "white angel." Mary Kay returned to the church for two years to teach Sunday School, and after that, she continued to support the church monetarily.

Mary Kay always had a tender spot in her heart for children, especially for those of sales force members who sent her letters asking for donations for causes in which they were involved, like mission trips, school activities, and various clubs. She always wrote a check when the request came from a child. One Valentine's Day, she loaded up her Cadillac with stuffed poodles named Gigi—in the likeness of her own dog—and delivered them to children in the hospitals around the Dallas area.

Mary Kay's commitment to young people and her consistent encouragement of them to dream was one of the reasons she attended the Horatio Alger Conference in Washington, D.C., every year. She felt it was important to participate in their program to encourage students. She would speak at the breakfast for students, where she would tell her story. The Horatio Alger Association presents scholarships to underprivileged students. As a member of the Scholarship Committee, Mary Kay read many applications and was always impressed with the abilities and tenacity of these students.

One of Mary Kay's ardent desires was that a cure for cancer be discovered in her lifetime. Because so many women in Mary Kay Inc. had been afflicted with cancer—and her husband Mel had died of lung cancer in 1980—Mary Kay was passionate about helping to fund a cure.

From 1987 until 1995, Mary Kay helped to raise over $2.5 million for cancer research. She believed that the only way to find a cure was through research, and she was always interested in research developments. One year, Mary Kay decided she could raise money by taking up a collection at the annual Seminar. This was a last-minute decision, and when she told the staff, they wanted to know how this could be done. She suggested that, like a church service, they pass the plate. When Mary Kay was told that there were no plates available, she decided they would use garbage bags. So the staff passed black garbage bags around the huge arena at the Dallas Convention Center at that year's Seminar. The next year, the staff anticipated Mary Kay's desire and had pink gift bags—printed with the words "Cancer Donations"—move across each row. Raising money at Seminar became a yearly tradition.

Mary Kay developed another unique way to raise money for cancer research. Because she was beloved by so many, she would receive thousands of Christmas and birthday cards each year. When she thought of how much those cards cost when added together, she realized that that money could significantly impact cancer research. Therefore, before her birthday and Christmas every year, Mary Kay would place a short request in the company publications asking sales force members to make a donation to cancer research in her name instead of sending a card or gift. As Mary Kay told the sales force when she asked for donations, "You never know. The dollar you give today could be the one that helps fund a breakthrough."

To assure that her fundraising efforts continued after she no longer led the company, Mary Kay founded the Mary Kay Ash Charitable Foundation in 1996, later renamed The Mary Kay Foundation (TMKF). She had two objectives in establishing this organization: to help women in need and to give others a vehicle to support the issues she held close to her heart. From its founding, TMKF awarded grants to fund innovative research studies across the United States for cancers affecting women, including ovarian, uterine, breast, and cervical cancers. In 1997, TMKF gave its first six cancer research grants of $100,000 each, for a total of $600,000. Today, TMKF gives ten to thirteen grants per year of $100,000 each to cancer research centers across the United States.

In 2000, the Foundation expanded its mission to help those organizations that prevent violence against women, another important issue that has impacted women in the Mary Kay sales force. When the Foundation adopted this objective, board members visited the National Domestic Violence Hotline in Austin, Texas, to ask the volunteers who manned the phones what they felt was the greatest need. Their response? "Keep the shelters open." The volunteers expressed their frustration at having a woman in danger on the other end of a phone call and being unable to find a safe place for her. Today, the Mary Kay Foundation grants $20,000 yearly to 150 women's shelters across the United States, for a total of three million dollars.

In addition to her financial resources, Mary Kay also gave her time. She never lost her ability to relate to the everyday things that women love, and she had great sympathy for the tragedies that many women experience. She made countless calls to those who were diagnosed with a serious disease or who had lost a loved one. Mary Kay tirelessly wrote get well and sympathy cards because she had such a heart for those who were hurting.

Mary Kay not only made people in the company feel important; she put this into practice in her community life. She was once asked to put her home on tour to raise money for charity, and she gave me two complimentary tickets to attend the tour with my mother. When we arrived at Mary Kay's house, she was greeting people at the front door. Of the five homes on the tour, Mary Kay was the only owner at home that day. She told me that if someone bought a ticket to see her home, she felt that they were also buying a ticket to meet her.

When Mary Kay traveled, flower bouquets from the hotel management, sales force members, and organizations with which she was interacting would often fill her room. On her way to the airport, she would always ask her driver to stop by a local hospital so she could donate the flowers to patients who didn't have any flowers to cheer them.

Mary Kay's philanthropic efforts extended throughout the world. Wherever Mary Kay Inc. has a subsidiary, the company encourages the practice of giving back to the community. In 2004—after Mary Kay's passing—I was privileged to attend an awards ceremony at Kensington Palace hosted by the People's Princess Charitable Foundation, Inc. Mary Kay and five other great humanitarians were to receive the Humanitarian Rose Award in the name of Princess Diana because they had founded organizations that touched lives in poor countries around the world.

I was asked to attend merely three days before the ceremony. Like Cinderella, my first thought was, "I have nothing to wear to the palace!" On the advice of my daughter, I ended up buying a gown that cost more than my wedding dress! The group of attendees and myself traveled down a long, tree-lined carriage drive and entered the Palace, where we descended a magnificent staircase. As I walked down, I was in full Cinderella fantasy mode, and like Proverbs warns, "Pride goes before destruction, and a haughty spirit before a fall." Four steps from the bottom of the staircase, I tripped and fell the rest of the way. I immediately stood up as if nothing had happened, but the palace guards had noticed my missteps and rushed to my side, asking me if I was alright. I desperately wanted to put this embarrassing moment behind me, but their concern lasted all evening as they periodically inquired about how I felt.

After viewing a collection of Princess Diana's formal gowns, we all climbed another spectacular staircase and were ushered to dinner in the King's Drawing Room, where, in ages past, the King hosted only his closest friends. After dinner, we were escorted to the Queen's

Gallery for a classical concert by the heads of three of the music departments from the London Symphony Orchestra. Seated in my petit point, high-backed chair, I expected Mr. Darcy from *Pride and Prejudice* to ask me for a dance.

When it came time to present the Humanitarian Rose Award, the founder of the People's Princess Charitable Foundation Inc., Maureen Dunkel, spoke about the purpose of the evening. She explained that this event was to honor six of the world's great humanitarians who shared a "common bond of compassion" and who "left a touch of love and compassion with those who need it most."

Mary Kay was primarily recognized for her vision of changing women's lives through the financial opportunities she gave women around the world and for her efforts to eradicate cancer through supporting research for the cure. Since the award was presented posthumously, her grandson Ryan Rogers accepted it on Mary Kay's behalf, telling the audience that she had built an organization of women who "live by the principles she held as the core of her philosophy . . . It is impossible to measure how many lives have been touched by the millions of women that followed in her footsteps and continue to carry on her mission today, but what is measurable is the global impact that is the legacy of Mary Kay Ash."

The evening ended with a final toast and pictures, and then recipients and guests were left to mingle. Dr. William and Mrs. Kathleen Magee, founders of Operation Smile and fellow award recipients, thanked me for the support that Mary Kay Russia had given to their organization. I was in awe: I had flown all the way to London, England, in 2004 to be thanked for the generosity of Mary Kay Russia, all because Mary Kay had followed her dream in Dallas, Texas, in 1963.

One of the greatest examples of Mary Kay's far-reaching charitable influence is in China, where Mary Kay China supports the Mary Kay Spring Bud Primary School. This school provides female students in a remote Chinese village with an opportunity to earn an education. I will never forget when Paul Mak, President of Mary Kay China, gave a presentation at a global conference in Dallas, Texas, for the United States and International staff. He showed a PowerPoint slide with Mary Kay's name written in English on a blackboard, with Chinese text underneath, which would tell the school girls about her.

Paul also told one anecdote that greatly affected me. The company held a special luncheon for the girls at the Spring Bud Primary School and presented the students with a feast of various meat dishes and rice. As the meal progressed, the Mary Kay staff noticed that the girls only ate their bowls of rice. When they asked one of the girls why this was so, she replied, "Only boys are allowed to eat meat." Paul then showed a slide of one little girl with an impish look on her face, her chopstick reaching for the meat. His story reminded me of how many people are presented with a glorious meal but don't take advantage of it because they see the limitations and not the permissions. As Mary Kay frequently remarked in her speeches, "You are invited to the banquet of life, and a place has been set for you. But you have to accept the invitation and take a seat."

As I watched Paul's presentation, I longed for Mary Kay to be sitting there instead of me so she could see the fruits of her labors. In 1963, she had planted a seed that has now reached remote areas around the world. What a testimony to someone who dedicated her life to living out Christian principles and sharing the love of Jesus.

In reflecting on the amazing philanthropic good Mary Kay achieved, I am reminded of a poem she especially loved, titled "A Bag of Tools" by R. L. Sharpe:

> Isn't it strange that princes and kings,
> And clowns that caper in sawdust rings,
> And common people like you and me

Are builders for eternity?
Each is given a bag of tools,
A shapeless mass,
A book of rules;
And each must make—
'Ere life has flown—
A stumbling block or a steppingstone.[2]

Mary Kay Inc. and The Mary Kay Foundation are stepping-stones that enrich women's lives. These organizations are built on a foundation of giving to others, knowing that in doing so, a person's life is blessed. As Mary Kay stated in her 1995 book *You Can Have It All*, "Do your kind deeds without expecting anything in return, and over the course of time, good will come back to you."[3]

8

MARY KAY THE STEWARD

As each has received a gift, use it to serve one another,
as good stewards of God's varied grace.

1 PETER 4:10

It has been said that rich people are just poor people with
money. The winner of a $5-million lottery is the same person
the day after he wins—except that he's $5 million richer. The
money will, of course, make a difference in his life. But if as
a result of his winnings he becomes arrogant, overbearing,
haughty, and self-important, he will lose the respect of others.

MARY KAY ASH[1]

Mary Kay believed in being a good steward of her money. She did not like debt, professionally or personally. For most of my years at Mary Kay Inc., the company was debt-free. There were times the company had to incur debt for its betterment, such as building their first manufacturing facility and financing a leveraged buyout in the mid-eighties, but any debts were always paid off as quickly as possible. This policy enabled Mary Kay Inc. to remain in good financial standing during the Great Recession of 2008.[2]

Maintaining a debt-free life was another of Mary Kay's policies. Even though a sales force member might have to take out a loan to invest in her original inventory, Mary Kay taught them a simple plan for putting their businesses on a cash basis by investing 60 percent of any profits back into the business. Mary Kay never wanted a sales force member to be burdened by her career because of her initial debt in purchasing her beginning inventory; she wanted them to be financially blessed. To ensure that the sales force practiced good financial principles, Mary Kay Inc. published a book on money management titled *Living a Rich Life: Achieving personal, financial and spiritual abundance following Mary Kay's laws of living rich.*[3]

In her personal life, Mary Kay was never frivolous. Anna Ewing, one of the pioneers of the company, said that Mary Kay never forgot her roots, was always on a diet, and always looked for a bargain.

For example, Anna recalled a story from a Sales Director who had earned a dinner with Mary Kay, and, although this Sales Director had never before bought expensive shoes, she wanted the evening to be special. She went out and purchased a pair of shoes for $150. When the Sales Director met Mary Kay, she wanted Mary Kay to notice her shoes, so she told Mary Kay how cute *her* shoes were. Mary Kay replied, "Do you like them? I found them for $19.95. I like them so much I went back and bought them in every other color."

Although Mary Kay felt it important to be stylish and appropriately dressed, she never sought to impress others with brand names or designer clothes. After she became so well known that she couldn't publicly shop without drawing a crowd, she ordered the Sales Director suits and National Sales Director suits in several colors; these became the core of her business wardrobe. She not only wore them to the office, but to interviews and onstage at Mary Kay meetings.

In the early years of Seminar, Mary Kay shopped for her Seminar gown at local department stores. One year, however, she and one of the National Sales Directors wore the same gown, so Mary Kay enlisted the services of a well-known American fashion designer

Victor Costa; he created gorgeous evening gowns specially made for her to wear onstage. Victor was aware of Mary Kay's thriftiness, and she liked the prices of his gowns.

Having her own designer became particularly important in the year Mary Kay had shingles around her waist and could not bear to wear any clothing that touched the rash. She knew the sales force was counting on her appearance at Seminar, and she didn't want to let them down. Mary Kay had Victor design her a pink, loose-fitting evening gown. Although her appearance on stage did not last long because of the pain, the attendees were grateful that she made the effort to show up.

When Mary Kay went shopping with top sales force members on their international award trips, she often concerned herself with their spending habits. On one such trip, Nan Stroud was looking at a jacket that cost six hundred dollars. She had never spent that much money on a piece of clothing, and when Mary Kay approached her, she confided her concern. "I told Mary Kay that I didn't know if I should get it because it was so expensive. She advised me, 'You really don't need to put your money into that. There are a lot better places to spend your money.'"

Even when Mary Kay traveled, she looked for bargains. Nancy Thomason recalls one of the first trips she took with Mary Kay as they crossed the country on the book tour for Mary Kay's autobiography. Driving from the airport to their hotel, Mary Kay noticed a five-and-dime store, and, after checking into the hotel, Mary Kay wanted to walk there. While they shopped, she stopped at the costume jewelry department and bought several items. She told Nancy, "Nobody knows the difference."

Mary Kay was always on the lookout for the best bargain on trips with Sales Directors and National Sales Directors. Once she found it, she would immediately share her discovery. As Cheryl Warfield said,

"She would sell us on the item with so much enthusiasm that we all couldn't wait to get one." Mary Kay even had some vendors come to her hotel suite with merchandise that she thought was a good deal, and she would invite others to shop with her.

Mary Kay was famous within the company for clipping coupons. In fact, it became a game to her to see how much money she could save at the grocery store. In the evening, I would often see Mary Kay waiting for the elevator with the grocery store ad in her hand after poring over it for the best bargains. She once expressed her excitement to me when she found an organization that exchanged coupons for items she did not use for those that she did.

On their way to the office one morning, Mary Kay enthusiastically said to Nancy, "I guess you heard about what happened yesterday." Since Mary Kay Inc. had experienced record-breaking sales the day before, Nancy responded, "Yes, wasn't it great?" Mary Kay's response was that it was indeed, because she had saved more in coupons at the grocery store than ever before.

Not only did Mary Kay clip coupons for herself, she also passed on coupons to others. One day, she brought a Whataburger coupon to an employee and said to him, "I noticed you were eating this hamburger at your desk yesterday. I thought you might like a coupon I have." Another time, she clipped a Grecian Formula coupon (a men's hair dye) for an executive who was graying and presented it to him.

Mary Kay loved saving money so much that she would bring me the rubber bands from her newspapers and insist, "We should never have to buy rubber bands at this company." These rubber bands were always so dirty and black from newspaper ink that I just couldn't use them for business purposes, so I made them into a rubber band ball.

Because of her Depression-Era mentality, Mary Kay could never reconcile what she thought were exorbitant prices in the business world. The staff learned that it was best to handle any charges discreetly rather than let Mary Kay see what the company had to pay for room service, restaurants, and catering charges. When staying in elite hotels, Mary Kay would have the staff bring in Chinese and Mexican food. She enjoyed staying on concierge floors because of the complimentary food and drinks they offered. In the morning, Mary Kay would send Nancy down for rolls, and what she didn't finish for breakfast she would eat later if she didn't have time for lunch.

The Mary Kay video production staff loved to tell the story about an experience they had at Mary Kay's house. They were there for an all-day shoot, and the company hired a catering service to provide snacks and lunch for the crew. After the food arrived, the catering company left the bill in the kitchen with Mary Kay's friend, who then handed it to Mary Kay. When Mary Kay saw the cost, she was horrified. She approached the manager of the project and told her she thought the charge was outrageous.

The manager explained that it was customary to feed the crew so that they would not have to leave the location and that catering costs were all planned within the budget. Mary Kay didn't care about that. All she knew was that this money came from the company coffers, and she felt the company was getting fleeced. Since this was to be a two-day shoot, she announced, "I will provide lunch tomorrow." The next day, the crew was treated to homemade pimento cheese sandwiches and chips, compliments of Mary Kay Ash.

Although the staff would laugh about stories of Mary Kay's thrifti-ness, they all knew that she was generous with others but careful with her own money. For instance, Mary Kay used coupons when she did her Christmas toy shopping—at the drug store. She would wait for the Christmas ad to arrive and then decide which toys she would purchase for each grandchild.

Mary Kay also loved rebates. If a store ran out of the advertised item, she always asked for a rebate. If someone went to the store for her and failed to get a rebate on an item that was out-of-stock, she always sent them back.

Mary Kay once found a product called "Shoe Makeup" that she used to color her old shoes to match an outfit in her closet. She also had a trick where she would color her diamond rings. Senior National Sales Director Emeritus Pat Danforth relates a time when she was at a dinner at Mary Kay's home with top staff and other top Sales Directors. She was seated almost directly across from Mary Kay and noticed her ring. It was a beautiful, pear-shaped ruby surrounded by many sparkling diamond baguettes. Except for the center stone, the ring was identical to a canary diamond ring Mary Kay's late husband Mel had given her, so Pat asked Mary Kay, "Do you have a ruby ring like your canary diamond one?"

When Mary Kay answered, "No," Pat brazenly asked her, "Is this a fashion ring?" Again, Mary Kay said, "No." Perplexed, Pat thought for a minute and remembered the plastic Pop-It Beads from the 1950s. She thought perhaps the stone came out and could be exchanged with the canary diamond. Again, Mary Kay said, "No." Finally, after a long pause, Mary Kay said, with a twinkle in her eye, "Magic Marker." Mary Kay explained that she learned this trick from her jeweler. He showed her that she could use a marker to change the color of a diamond, and then later remove the color with a cotton swab and nail polish remover. Pat confessed that she has used this trick dozens of times to make faux rubies, emeralds, sapphires, amethysts, and even onyx.[4]

When Mary Kay and Mel built their round house, Mary Kay was urged to take out a loan. She hated making the monthly payments when she knew she could just pay it off—so she did. Then, in the early 1980s, the top National Sales Directors in the company started making six-figure commissions. Many of them began building their dream homes, and they would send notes full of gratitude, along with pictures, to Mary Kay. One afternoon, I saw her looking at some of these pictures. She glanced at me and said, "These homes are fabulous. Do you think I need a bigger house?"

It wasn't too long after this conversation that Mary Kay went house hunting. She looked at numerous mansions for sale in the Dallas area, but none of them suited her. Mary Kay then saw a huge house with a pink exterior and fell in love . . . but it was under construction. She talked to the builder, who told Mary Kay that she could finish it out and decorate it according to her tastes. This prospect excited her, and she impetuously bought the stucco house without researching the builder. Like most women, she loved the experience of choosing the wall colors, fixtures, flooring, and furniture. She even went to Paris to select a few accent pieces.

The house was magnificent, with six bedrooms, a library, and a media room. There were six full and two half bathrooms, one of which included a pink quartz toilet and bathtub. One of its three living areas featured forty-foot-high ceilings. An Olympic-sized swimming pool dominated the backyard.

Mary Kay wanted to have the construction completed and to be fully moved into the home by Seminar so she could host the top winners there. And she made it—barely. Crews worked on the house almost to the moment when the first buses of winners rolled up to the gate.

Mary Kay was excited to show off her pink castle. Although July is a hot, arid month in Dallas, as her first group of visitors arrived, it started raining, and she discovered that the builder did not seal any of the windows. Mary Kay's floor-to-ceiling, pink silk drapes in the great room were completely ruined. Water poured through the ceiling from the library upstairs, and Mary Kay and her staff ran around with towels and pots trying to halt the damage. Unfortunately, there were so many leaks that they finally gave up. Later that night, Mary Kay was walking down the hall on the second floor when the dry wall fell through. All kinds of trash—including lunch bags and uneaten food—fell onto the floor.

This day just marked the beginning of the problems with the house. Electric wires were found unconnected. A creek that flowed under the foundation seeped up onto the first level of the house and a sump tank had to be installed to keep the house from flooding. On top of all these problems, the contractor had not paid his workers, who had started showing up at Mary Kay's house demanding money—which Mary Kay gave them. Her lawyers advised against this, but as Mary Kay told Nancy, the workers had families to feed, and she had great concern for them.

Mary Kay also discovered that big houses incur big expenses. One day, she exclaimed to me in distress, "I just got my electric bill, and it was over $1,600!" I was shocked. "Mary Kay," I said, "That is more than what most people spend on their mortgage in a month." She immediately made changes to how she used electricity, and she started turning off the air conditioners in all parts of the house that she didn't use. She would only turn them on when she had events at her home, and then only after she heard that her guests were on the way.

The house eventually became too much for a woman living alone. Something was always breaking, and Mary Kay dreaded going home. She wanted out. She had never sold the round house that she and Mel had built. In 1990, she couldn't bear to live in the mansion any longer, and she made the decision to move back into her former home that was filled with warm memories. She was happy there. Mary Kay later told me, "I succumbed to peer pressure. All the National Sales Directors were buying big houses, and so I thought I should have one too." Simple living was her preferred lifestyle.

Moving from a twelve-thousand-square-foot mansion back to her comfy, smaller house required major downsizing, so Mary Kay decided to hold a garage sale. She posted signs and told everyone she met about the big sale she was having at her home. She had always loved selling, and she was as excited as a child opening her first lemonade stand.

Mary Kay had already moved back to her round house on the day of the garage sale, but she wanted to arrive at the pink house early to make sure everything was set up on time. She and Nancy got there before the sun had risen, but as they neared the house, they saw such a long line of cars that they couldn't tell where it ended. Mary Kay was gleeful. "I think we're going to sell everything!" Of course, sales force members had jumped at the chance to get a glimpse of Mary Kay's pink mansion and to buy an item she had personally owned. One staff member stocked up on Mary Kay's purses to use for prizes whenever she held Mary Kay meetings.

Mary Kay took to heart the words in the parable of the talents, found in Matthew 25:14–30. As she often said, "It tells us to use and increase whatever God has given us, and that when we do, we shall be given more. I deeply believe in this philosophy, and I've always applied it throughout my business career."

9

THE MARY KAY CULTURE

Keep my teaching as the apple of your eye.

PROVERBS 7:2B

Many of the unpleasant experiences in my previous career taught me the rules for dealing with people.

MARY KAY ASH[1]

Over the years, Mary Kay developed a company culture based on her philosophies and teachings. The corporate goal has always been to preserve these teachings. For thirty-three years, Mary Kay was in the office daily, and she was the living example of the Mary Kay culture. If there were any questions about the right thing to do, the staff could go to Mary Kay for the answer. But, after she could no longer be present due to her health, and as new managers and new employees were hired, the company saw the need to establish a permanent committee for perpetuating Mary Kay's ideals.

The culture committee was formed in response to the challenge of keeping the culture alive and special among Mary Kay Inc. employees. Serving on this committee was one of the roles I enjoyed the most. The National Sales Directors had been delegated by Mary Kay to carry on her principles with the sales force, and they admirably stepped into this assignment.

Mary Kay was loyal to her people, both on the staff and the sales force. She knew the importance of employee loyalty and tenure for a company's success. Many know the common saying, "People are known by the company they keep." But Mary Kay would say, "A company is known by the people it keeps." While Alfred P. Sloan, a famous CEO of General Motors, insisted, "Take my assets but leave me my organization, and in five years I will have it back," Mary Kay would say, "Take our assets and leave the people whose seeds of greatness are being nurtured in a Golden Rule workplace, and we can do it all again."

Since Mary Kay had amassed twenty-five years of experience in the direct selling industry, she used its marketing model when she began her company. For that reason, Mary Kay Inc. was always—and continues to be—an active member of the Direct Selling Association (DSA). One of Mary Kay's goals was that her company be an example and influence for other companies. Having started her career as a saleswoman, she valued the contributions of the sales force. She vowed that every decision she made would be to their benefit.

With her experience and unique principles, Mary Kay built an organization based on integrity, honesty, and quality. The result? Mary Kay Inc. soon became a leader in the direct selling industry.[2] The company and Mary Kay Ash's legacy are highly respected among its direct selling peers: Mary Kay Ash, Mary Kay Inc., and other key executives within the organization have received numerous DSA awards and have often served as officers, board members, and members of important DSA committees. Notably, Mary Kay was inducted into the DSA Hall of Fame in 1976. She also received both the Circle of Honor Award in 1989 and the Living Legend Award in 1992 from the Direct Selling Education Foundation.

Mary Kay Inc.'s culture and tradition set the company apart from others because of the exemplary principles she established right from the start.

THE MARY KAY IMAGE

Image was vital to Mary Kay. When she started the company in 1963, the direct selling industry had a questionable image, and Mary Kay was determined to change that perception. She developed what came to be known as the "Mary Kay Image," which included how a Beauty Consultant looked and acted. Mary Kay would tell the sales force, "You never get a second chance to make a good first impression." Her goal was to build a prestigious, well-dressed, and well-groomed sales force.

An amusing true story from the early days of the company illustrates why Mary Kay tried to impress the importance of image on the sales force. In the late 1960s, a popular Dallas columnist wrote an article for the front page of his newspaper that caused quite a furor. While driving to work, he had noticed a bumper sticker with the message, "Ask Me About Mary Kay Cosmetics." The woman driving the car was wearing a bathrobe, had her hair in rollers, and wore no makeup, prompting the columnist to question just how qualified she was to advise anyone on how to be beautiful.

His article appeared on a Monday morning, and by 7:00 a.m., Mary Kay's phone was ringing with people wanting to know if she had seen the story. At this time, Mary Kay Cosmetics was still small, with most sales force members living in and around Dallas (where the company was headquartered). The sales force used the company conference rooms, and Monday mornings were a popular meeting time. Mary Kay immediately pinned the article to a bulletin board in a common space and wrote above it in big, bold letters: "WAS THIS YOU?" She later sent the article to sales force members outside of Dallas to reinforce the importance of the "Mary Kay Image." As she would remind those who worked with her, "Your actions speak so loudly that I can't hear what you are saying."

One of the first things Mary Kay did at her company was introduce career apparel. She asked her sales force to always look professional and to wear dresses or skirts, as she felt women could be simultaneously successful and feminine. The company initially offered apparel to the Beauty Consultants because, at its start, the entire sales force consisted of Beauty Consultants. However, as the company began promoting women to the role of Sales Director, Mary Kay wanted them to stand out as models of professionalism and style. She discontinued the Beauty Consultant apparel and started making suits for those women who earned the title of Sales Director. For nine consecutive years, the Sales Director suits earned the top apparel honors from the Career Apparel Institute, and the organization awarded Mary Kay Inc. the "Career Apparel of the Decade Award" for the 1980s.

Mary Kay always chose the final suit, but she left it up to apparel experts within the company to research fashion trends and select the correct fabrics. Each year, the apparel department would give a "fashion show" for Mary Kay in her office—with staff members modeling the different options—and present her with three or four suit styles and colors from which she would pick her favorite. She would often combine what she saw with her own ideas, such as fabric from one suit with the jacket from another and then a different skirt design from yet another. These suits became a symbol of success among the Mary Kay sales force, and Beauty Consultants aspired to the day when they could wear one.

One of my personal "wow" moments in the company took place at the first Leadership Conference I attended. The entire arena was filled with Mary Kay Sales Directors, all wearing the same lavender suit. As I stood by the stage and looked out upon a sea of lilac, I couldn't help but think of the sheer number of leaders in that room and all the power Mary Kay had unleashed within those women to inspire and motivate others.

Mary Kay Inc. began promoting career apparel again at the sales force level in 1973 after Mary Kay attended a baseball game. Mary

Kay had a passion for raising money for cancer research, and this goal grew in 1971 when breast cancer took the life of Eileen Sullivan, the first Sales Director to lose a battle with this disease. Eileen's sister-in-law, National Sales Director Emeritus Ann Sullivan, was also a Sales Director at the time, and Kathe Cunningham, the wife of the Community Relations Manager for the St. Louis Cardinals, happened to be one of Ann's offspring Sales Directors.[3] Kathe and her husband Joe discussed the possibility of having a Mary Kay night at the ballpark to benefit cancer research. In promoting the event, Joe discovered that fans were excited to attend a game that featured pink Cadillacs and "pretty women in skirts."

Joe ordered pink jerseys for the players and had a custom pair of pink shoes made for himself. He also asked Mary Kay to throw out the first pitch of the game. When Mary Kay arrived, Joe asked her if she would like to practice, but as soon as he handed Mary Kay the glove and ball, he realized they might have a problem: Mary Kay put the glove on the wrong hand! Fortunately, when the big moment came, her pitch *almost* made it to home plate.

There were other festivities on the field to celebrate "Mary Kay Night." Besides a pink Cadillac parade, the top team builders on the sales force donned red jackets to honor the Cardinals and lined up along the first and third baselines. When Mary Kay stepped on the field, those red jackets immediately caught her attention.

Mary Kay was so excited about the idea of red jackets for team builders that she immediately pitched this concept to others. From St. Louis, she headed out to California, making several other stops. At each city, she couldn't stop talking about the red jackets in St. Louis. The idea quickly spread across the country. Mary Kay realized it was time to develop a company program, and in 1981, the "TLC Red Jacket" program officially launched. The program earned this name because Mary Kay wanted to remind the sales force that leadership positions at Mary Kay Inc. require tender, loving care to bring new sales force members into the company.

Mary Kay not only stressed the importance of appearance to the sales force, but she thought that the Mary Kay staff should project a happy and welcoming image. She loved to tell the story of a businessman who came into the corporate offices one day and took a seat in the lobby. He didn't say anything, so after several minutes, the receptionist asked, "Sir, can I help you with something?" He responded that he had just come into the lobby to get his "battery recharged." He was impressed with the smiling, welcoming people who worked in the Mary Kay offices, and he liked coming to the Mary Kay building because everyone was so friendly and professional.

I had a similar experience when I attended a student banquet with one of my children. I was seated next to a gentleman who, when he learned I was employed by Mary Kay Inc., praised the company's receptionist, Janette Scott. He told me that she was the best receptionist in Dallas. He was exuberant about Janette's friendliness and enthusiasm for the company, but what impressed him most was that she not only greeted him with a big smile, but also remembered his name.

The human relations department was on the ground floor next to Janette's desk. When their regular receptionist went on maternity leave, the company hired a temporary to fill her job. Janette advised the temp that, when Mary Kay came into the building, she would first say hello to Janette and then turn and acknowledge the receptionist in human resources. Janette advised the temp to keep a smile on her face, and if Mary Kay asked her how she was doing, she was to say, "Mary Kay, I'm doing great!" There was a picture of Mary Kay in the lobby, and Janette showed it to the temp so she would know who Mary Kay was when she arrived. Sure enough, upon entering the building, Mary Kay greeted Janette and then turned and greeted the temp, but the new girl simply stared back at Mary Kay and never responded. Needless to say, May Kay was upset because she insisted that everyone who walked into the Mary Kay building be acknowledged warmly.

THE PINK CADILLAC

Mary Kay became a household name in America partially because of the pink Cadillacs that she and her top Sales Directors drove. The pink Cadillac program originated in 1968, when Mary Kay needed a new car. She had driven a Cadillac since 1951 and was a loyal Cadillac customer. In fact, her childhood nickname was "Caddy," so it was only natural that Mary Kay went to her Cadillac dealer for a new car.

She took a Mary Kay Cosmetics pink lip and eye compact with her and told the dealer she wanted her new Cadillac painted that same shade of pink. He tried to talk her out of the idea, telling her she would be back within two weeks asking to have her pink car repainted in its original color. Mary Kay was insistent, and the dealer complied. Her new pink Cadillac created a sensation on the streets of Dallas. Mary Kay joked that when she came to an intersection, "the waters parted," and she was waved through. Parking lot attendants put her car at the front of their lots so everyone who passed by could see it. Invariably, a crowd gathered around Mary Kay's pink Cadillac.

The first time Mary Kay drove her pink Cadillac to the office, the entire sales force wanted one. Sales Directors contacted Mary Kay's Cadillac dealer to purchase one just like hers, and pink Cadillacs filled the Mary Kay parking lot in no time. Mary Kay and her son Richard reasoned that, if the Sales Directors were willing to purchase a Cadillac with their own money, they would also be willing to earn one. In 1969, the company awarded the first five pink Cadillacs to the top five Sales Directors. The next year the company gave away ten, and in the next two years they gave away twenty.

Anna Ewing came in at number twenty-one on the final year the company gave away twenty Cadillacs to the top twenty Sales Directors. Disappointed that she had come so close, Anna met with Richard and asked him if he could figure out how much it would take to earn a pink Cadillac and make it available to everyone who qualified at that level. The company then made a momentous decision—instead of giving the cars to a set number of people every year, any Sales Director could earn a pink Cadillac at a certain production level.

The next year, the number of Cadillacs the company gave away rose from twenty to fifty-two! While some Sales Directors felt that they could never be in the top twenty in the nation, they knew they could stretch to meet a specific, numbers-based goal. The company was on its way to being what Mary Kay called "a pink car-nation!" Over time, the pink Cadillac—which Mary Kay called "a trophy on wheels"—became known as the company's most visual symbol of success. A parking lot owner in New Jersey even wrote to Mary Kay after he had the pleasure of having two pink Cadillacs parked on his lot one day. He experienced the greatest publicity he had ever seen, so he told Mary Kay that he would be happy to keep a pink Cadillac polished, shined, and washed if she would like him to permanently display one in his lot.

Mary Kay was often teased about the pink Cadillac and was asked by numerous interviewers why she would choose the color. Her answer was, "And what color of car does your boss give you?" Whenever people learn I worked for Mary Kay, the first question they always ask is, "Did you drive a pink Cadillac?" Of course I didn't, since pink Cadillacs are reserved for top Sales Directors and National Sales Directors.

As the years passed, one of the craziest rumors circulating about the pink Cadillac was that it was originally going to be a pink Lincoln. This urban legend is probably based on a story Mary Kay tells in her autobiography about the time she wanted to purchase a black and white Ford, but instead came home with a yellow Mercury. This happened in the forties, when women did not go by themselves to purchase big-ticket items like cars.

Car salesmen at that time were accustomed to dealing with the "man of the house." Mary Kay had saved her money until she could pay cash for the car, so the car she drove to the showroom was old and well-worn. The Ford salesman dismissed her as a potential customer when he saw her getting out of her rundown car, and when she asked to speak to the manager, the salesman told her that the manager would not be back for another hour.

Since she had the time, Mary Kay decided to visit the Mercury dealer across the street, and a yellow Mercury in their showroom caught her eye. It was more expensive than the Ford, but she liked it. When she told the salesman there that she was giving herself a new car as a birthday gift, he excused himself for a few minutes and came back with a bouquet of roses, wishing her a happy birthday. His customer service won her over, and Mary Kay drove home in a yellow Mercury that day instead of in a black and white Ford.

THE ADOPTEE PROGRAM

The Adoptee Program, which consists of "adopting" Beauty Consultants from other Sales Directors, grew out of Mary Kay's effort to solve the problem of territories. At one point in her career, Mary Kay moved from Houston to St. Louis. She had built a large base in Houston, but she lost it when she moved. Someone else was reaping the benefits of her hard work. Mary Kay wanted to create a fairer way to treat people who had to move, so she developed a program where there was no recruiting or selling territories. For this to work, Sales Directors across the United States would welcome team members of other Sales Directors into their meetings and treat them as their own without receiving any compensation for their efforts.

For example, a Sales Director in Dallas could arrange for a Sales Director in Houston to adopt one of her Beauty Consultants and invite her to attend sales meetings and participate in her events. As Mary Kay pointed out, "Remember, it's a two-way street. While a Sales Director may adopt somebody in her city, it's just as likely that one of her Consultants will be adopted somewhere else. Over a period of time, the efforts average out."[4]

The Adoptee Program is especially important when a Beauty Consultant moves away from her Sales Director and finds continued support and camaraderie among Mary Kay people in her new area. Many people thought the Adoptee Program would not work, but it did, and it is still one of the cornerstones of the Mary Kay marketing plan.

Go-Give

Mary Kay developed a unique philosophy called the Go-Give Program. Go-Give means to give unselfishly to others with no thought of remuneration. The foundation of the Go-Give Spirit is the desire to help others.

The Go-Give and Adoptee Programs work hand-in-hand. The Go-Give Award was officially launched in 1973 as a monthly program that recognized Directors for their willingness to help any Consultant or Director climb the ladder of success, especially through the Adoptee Program. Nominated by their peers, each winner of the Go-Give Award is chosen by a committee at corporate headquarters for possessing the qualities of warmth, love, giving, and caring.

The first example of a woman who demonstrated these qualities within Mary Kay Cosmetics was Sue Z. Vickers, the company's sixth

National Sales Director. Mary Kay called her, "the original Miss Go-Give." In 1971, Sue Z. was the first and only Mary Kay salesperson to be honored as Miss Mary Kay Image, the predecessor to the Go-Give Award. Mary Kay Inc. Sales Directors view the Go-Give Award as the top company award because it rewards character rather than achievement. In 1978, the first annual Go-Give Award was presented at Seminar as a memorial to Sue Z., whose tragic murder in the same year left a tremendous void in the Mary Kay Inc. sales force and Mary Kay's heart. To honor Sue Z.'s memory, Mary Kay planted an Austrian pine tree at the company headquarters.

Everyone in the company who knew Sue Z. agreed that she was one of the most giving and caring people one could meet. She was friendly and gave generously of her time and knowledge. Sue Z. was also a great motivator. She would walk around meetings in a long, flowing robe, carrying a wand. If someone came up to her and said, "Sue Z., teach me how to book beauty shows," she would tap them on the head and say, "You can book now." Her speeches were a lot of fun and full of action. She would have everyone in the audience stand and say, "I'm not a chicken, I'm not a chicken! I'm a superstar, I'm a superstar!" with appropriate accompanying gestures, of course!

As a new Beauty Consultant, Cheryl Warfield recalls the first class she attended under Sue Z.'s teaching. Cheryl had a background as a calculus teacher and preferred things to be logical and realistic. Sue Z. told her class that she was going to give them the secret to success. She had them stand up and climb on top of their chairs because they were not high enough. They needed to get closer to God.

"You have to wake up your genie," Sue Z. always told people. "If you don't feel your genie is awake, then pound on your chest. And just in case that doesn't awaken your genie, yell '*Yahoo*! My sleeping genie is alive!'" At that point, she had everyone put their hands up in a "V" shape to "catch the abundance God wanted to give them."

Cheryl thought these instructions were bizarre. She then thought that perhaps she did need to reach for God's abundance and quit being so negative. As she loves to tell people today, Cheryl has attended many classes over her career, but this is the only one that she remembers word for word.

Sue Z. was known for her positive attitude. She never believed in gossiping, and she treated everyone with respect. She was completely loyal to the company. At the first National Sales Director Summit at the Tan-Tar-A hunting lodge in Osage Beach, Missouri, the National Sales Directors met informally to chat after the meeting was over. When the women began discussing things that they thought the company should change, Sue Z. sat there quietly and then reminded them that they worked for a company that was good to them and that they should support it 100 percent. She pointed out that the company was young, was on the verge of great growth, and that it gave them the opportunity to touch people's lives.

RECOGNITION AND PRIZES

Mary Kay believed in praising people to success. As she stated in her autobiography, "Let people know that you appreciate them and their performance, and they'll respond by doing even better. Applause and the recognition it represents are among the world's most powerful forces."[5]

Mary Kay knew that there were many types of motivation, and prizes were one of them. As a young saleswoman, Mary Kay learned the importance of giving the right prize. Her sales manager had run a contest and kept teasing his salespeople, who were women, about how great the prize was. Mary Kay loved prizes, and she worked very hard to win. However, for all her efforts, she was awarded a flounder light for gigging fish in a river at night. She was dumbstruck: "Why would anyone think a woman would want a flounder light for a present?"

After that experience, Mary Kay determined that, if she were to give women prizes, she would give them what she called "Cinderella" prizes—items that women want but would not normally buy for themselves, such as diamond jewelry. She did not consider monetary gifts as Cinderella prizes. As Mary Kay explained it, most women would spend that money on their families before they would buy something nice for themselves. The women who received Cinderella prizes worked for a full year to earn them, and the prizes were awarded at Seminar. Over the years, the Cinderella prizes have evolved into designer items as well as impressive trips and cars.

Mary Kay Inc. also offers smaller consistency prizes for the sales force. Independent Beauty Consultants can earn these prizes every quarter. The first consistency prize Mary Kay offered was a golden goblet. In one of her previous direct sales companies, she worked hard every month to earn a miniature, plastic, silver-colored loving cup. She valued these cups and kept them all her life. Mary Kay believed that if she had strived so hard for such an impractical prize, the sales force would work to earn a goblet they could proudly display at their dinner tables. When she brought up the idea to her son Richard, he told her the idea would never work, but since she oversaw sales force motivation, it was her call.

The Golden Goblet Award was introduced in 1966. Mary Kay conceived the award to recognize exceptional activity and inspire consistency—winners had to generate $1,000 wholesale a month. Some Mary Kay staff members were skeptical that sales force members could attain such a lofty goal, as $1,000 wholesale a month was a level of production that was unheard of at that time. A sales force member would have to sell $2,000 retail. The basic skin care set was $15.95, and the complete set—which included glamour—was $24.00.

As an added incentive, the company announced that there would be a banquet at Seminar for every goblet winner and an opportunity to take a picture with Mary Kay and Mel under a "Golden Goblet" banner. To everyone's surprise, the promotion was an unbelievable success, with over three hundred winners. Mary Kay and Mel stood at the entrance of the banquet hall. Dressed in elegant gowns and high heels, winners patiently stood in line to have their pictures taken with the couple. Over two hours passed before everyone was seated. The first goblet winners jokingly called that event "the bunion parade."

Over time, Beauty Consultants who consistently earned a goblet each month started running out of room to store and display them. The company then decided to add the option of fine china. The program expanded, and independent sales force members were given a choice of either a goblet or a place setting. Designed exclusively for Mary Kay Inc., the china featured delicate gold filigree on a pink border. After one winner reached eighty-nine consecutive months of goblet status, though, Mary Kay and Richard realized that they needed a new incentive award. The goblet program was replaced with a gold ladder piece of jewelry, to which sales force members could add gemstone stars for their monthly achievements. The gems included diamonds, sapphires, and rubies and were based on the individual's production level.

In her speeches, Mary Kay often told the story of the bumblebee. Aerodynamic engineers have said that the bumblebee should not be able to fly because its wings are too weak and its body too heavy. Mary Kay would add, "Fortunately, the bumblebee doesn't know that, and it goes right on flying." Mary Kay felt that this creature was the perfect symbol for women who reached the top in the company, as many of them had been told that they would never be a success. One of the most popular company prizes is a diamond bumblebee pin. The original pin was a Thursday present that Mel gave to Mary Kay. Mary

Kay and Mel were married on a Thursday, and on the first Thursday after they were married, he brought her a present to celebrate their one-week anniversary. Mary Kay, being the smart woman that she was, asked him, "You mean you're going to do this every week?"[6] Thus began the tradition of Mel bringing Mary Kay a present every Thursday for the rest of their fourteen-year marriage. These gifts ranged from something as simple as chocolates to exquisite items, one of which was highlighted in *Only the Best,* a book featuring the favorite gifts received by famous people. For that book, Mary Kay chose to talk about a Cybis porcelain Madonna bust inscribed with, "To A Living Madonna From A Loving and Devoted Husband."

Mary Kay loved her diamond bumblebee Thursday present. She always had an eye for what would motivate the sales force, and she immediately told Mel that she felt everyone would want one. Mary Kay decided that the diamond bumblebee would make a fitting prize for the queens of each of the Mary Kay courts. It became so popular that smaller bees were given to the Court of Sharing in 1972. Over the years, the bee has been redesigned to stay modern and has been issued in limited edition forms, such as pink diamonds. It is a coveted symbol of success in the Mary Kay world. Some women have won so many bees that they boast a "swarm" on their shoulders.

One of my most prized possessions is the bumblebee ring Mary Kay Ash gave to me on my twentieth anniversary with the company. At that time, only sales force members could wear the bee pin, so Mary Kay took a bee from her personal collection and brought it to her jeweler. She asked him if he could make it into a ring for me. Many years later, earning a bumblebee ring became an option for sales force members, but I am proud to say that I was the first woman at Mary Kay Inc. to own one.

However, May Kay also realized that she didn't have to give expensive prizes to motivate people. She taught everyone that a word of encouragement, appreciation, and belief can be as motivational as any prize. One of her frequent sayings was, "A forty cent prize given with one hundred dollars' worth of recognition is a thousand times more effective than a one-hundred-dollar prize given with forty cents' worth of recognition."

The Number Thirteen

As the success of the company grew, Mary Kay began regarding the number thirteen as her significant number. She had launched her company on Friday the thirteenth, and after that, the number thirteen kept showing up throughout her life. In 1976, Mary Kay became the thirteenth inductee into the Direct Selling Association's Hall of Fame in the thirteenth year the award was given. In 1983, she was the thirteenth awardee of the Entrepreneur of the Year Award from Southern Methodist University's Edwin L. Cox School of Business.

Mary Kay's first manufacturing facility operated at 1330 Regal Row for thirty years. The Mary Kay headquarters in Addison has thirteen stories and thirteen elevators, which thrilled Mary Kay when the company was in the market for a new location. The building's previous owner didn't want a thirteenth floor, so they referred to it as the penthouse. Mary Kay was proud to announce that her office was on the thirteenth floor.

Once thirteen became such an important number for Mary Kay, the company began to plan momentous Mary Kay events on the thirteenth day of the month, including its first Seminar. Subsidiaries often opened on the thirteenth, and the *On Silver Wings* sculpture by artist Norman Boyles, created in honor of the famous poem that she loved so much, was unveiled on the company's twenty-fifth anniversary, September 13, 1988.

NEW DIRECTOR TRADITIONS

Whenever a Beauty Consultant rises to the level of Sales Director, she attends an orientation week in Dallas. Over the years, several traditions evolved that make this week special for participants—one of the most unusual was having a photograph taken in Mary Kay's bathtub. This strange rite of passage began in 1969 when Mary Kay and Mel first moved into their round house and invited the Sales Directors to tour their new home.

Mary Kay opened every room in her house and invited everyone to take pictures. She had installed a sunken marble tub in her bathroom, and the Sales Directors were enthralled by it. Two of them decided that it would be fun to get in the bathtub and take pictures, and soon everyone was jumping in for photos. After that, whenever Mary Kay hosted events for the sales force at her home, attendees insisted on taking their bathtub pictures. When the new Sales Director orientation classes became so large that Mary Kay could no longer host them in her home, the company purchased a pink, heart-shaped bathtub purely for the photo op. Today, the tub is displayed in The Mary Kay Museum during new Sales Director events.

Another tradition that Mary Kay started with the new Sales Directors was to serve tea and cookies that she personally made. She served a cold spiced tea made with sweetener, and her collection of cookie recipes was quite extensive. She had several "regulars," including "Wham-Bam" cookies and oatmeal crisps.[7] The company eventually published a cookie recipe book with all of Mary Kay's favorites, which was presented as a gift to the new Sales Directors.

These two traditions have continued to this day. When new Sales Directors visit the Dallas headquarters during their orientation week, they can hop into the pink, heart-shaped bathtub for a photograph taken by a Mary Kay staff member and enjoy cookies made with Mary Kay's recipes.

The Warm Fuzzy

During the late 1970s and 1980s, fuzzy pink puffballs with antennas, googly eyes, and purple feet adorned many desks in the offices at the Mary Kay headquarters. These were Mary Kay's "warm fuzzies," based on a book called *The Original Warm Fuzzy Tale* by Claude Steiner.[8] Mary Kay first heard this story when she visited Minneapolis in 1974; Sales Director Helene Reiner, who eventually became a National Sales Director, used the illustration in a speech. The book told the story of a hidden valley filled with people who were always happy because they gave each other "warm fuzzies" that signified their care for one another. Mary Kay loved the story so much that she decided to use it in her Seminar speech that year.

Impressed by this tale, Mary Kay commissioned a manufacturer to make little pink fuzzies that she and her sales force members could pass out. She distributed them at Seminar, and the sales force could order them year-round. Soon, pink fuzzies could be spotted throughout the Mary Kay building.

Mary Kay Inc.'s traditions were ultimately all a product of its culture that set this company apart from other firms in the industry. The traditions embodied May Kay's philosophy and promoted her principles of doing business and have continued to do so to this day.

Seminar

Of course, the most important and impressive tradition is the annual Seminar held in Dallas, Texas, every summer. It is the highlight of the Mary Kay year when sales force achievers are awarded recognition and prizes for their accomplishments. It also has elements of education, inspiration, and motivation.

Mary Kay knew firsthand how important this type of meeting was for a salesperson's success. She attended her very first event of this kind when she was a new dealer with Stanley Home Products. Her party average was seven dollars, and she knew she had a lot to learn, but it cost twelve dollars to attend. Mary Kay didn't have the money, so she had to borrow it. She was then lectured on how irresponsible she was to be spending this money on a trip to Dallas instead of on clothes for her children.

Two things happened at the Stanley meeting that impacted Mary Kay's career. Firstly, she saw another Stanley dealer crowned "Stanley Queen," and the woman was awarded an alligator handbag. Mary Kay then set a goal for herself: she would earn the title of queen and win one of those purses. She introduced herself to that year's "Stanley Queen" and asked the woman if she would mind showing Mary Kay how she held a party, to which the woman agreed. Mary Kay took nineteen pages of notes during their conversation, which she immediately put into practice upon returning home. She called these notes her "railroad to success."

Secondly, Mary Kay marched up to the president of Stanley and told him that next year, she would be queen. His reply to her was, "Somehow, I think you will be." She held on to his remarks as she worked hard each month and increased her sales to the point where she did attain the throne. Unfortunately, an alligator handbag was not awarded that year. She was, however, satisfied that she had met her goal and had provided for her family through direct sales.

Years later, at Mary Kay Inc.'s thirtieth anniversary, a Stanley executive who had worked with Mary Kay when she was a young saleswoman came to Seminar and personally delivered an alligator handbag to her. He said, "Mary Kay considers this handbag to be the prize that got away. At Stanley, we consider the prize that got away to be Mary Kay." In her autobiography, Mary Kay commented, "Well, I never considered myself a prize—just an ordinary woman with extraordinary determination."[9]

Many of the traditions incorporated into the Mary Kay culture came from Mary Kay's experiences in other direct selling companies. One of these traditions involved Seminar. When she had to borrow the money for that first seminar with Stanley Home Products, Mary Kay did not have extra funds for food, so she packed a pound of cheese and a box of crackers in her suitcase. When others in attendance would make lunch and dinner plans, she excused herself and went to her hotel room to eat her cheese and crackers. Mary Kay realized that she missed some wonderful opportunities for networking and sharing ideas with other attendees, so when she started putting together programs for Mary Kay Cosmetics, she included breakfast and lunch as part of the registration cost. She didn't want others to feel excluded like she had. This meant that as the company grew, Mary Kay Inc. fed about seven thousand to eight thousand sales force members during the Seminar lunch breaks.

The very first Mary Kay Seminar was held in 1964, on the company's first anniversary. Seminar had a meager beginning and was hosted at the company's warehouse. Decorations included crepe paper and balloons—which Mary Kay hung herself—and Mary Kay personally cooked and deboned chicken for two hundred guests. The meal included a gelatin salad that melted on everyone's plate because of the Texas September heat. Entertainment was provided by an opera singer whose mother was a Beauty Consultant. Dinner was followed by the recognition of the top salespeople, with the big prize being a black-and-white television. Afterward, Mary Kay stayed to take down the decorations and clean up the warehouse.

Sing-a-longs were another big part of the early Seminars. From her experiences at church and the meetings she had attended with other direct selling companies, Mary Kay knew that singing could set the mood and bring joy to the heart. After the first few Seminars, she decided the company would have a song contest; the winning songs would be added to the program for the next year's Seminar. Sales force members wrote lyrics to the tunes of "Take Me Out to the Ball Game" and "Clementine." The most popular song was to the tune of an old camp-meeting hymn, "I've Got That Joy, Joy, Joy, Joy Down in My Heart," which became, "I've Got That Mary Kay Enthusiasm Down in My Heart." For years, this song was sung not only at company events but also at the openings of local meetings around the country.

No alcohol is ever served at Mary Kay meetings, including Seminar. There are several reasons for this. Back in the 1960s, many women had to have permission from their husbands to attend an out-of-city event. Husbands were more at ease knowing that there would be no alcohol at Mary Kay Inc. events. If they still had doubts, husbands have always been invited to Mary Kay Inc. meetings to facilitate their understanding of the company's principles and integrity, and to support their wives.

The second reason the company doesn't serve alcohol at Seminar stemmed from an experience Mary Kay had at a former direct selling company. As an award one year, that company took its top salespeople on a Hawaiian vacation. Cocktails were served, including mai tais. One of the most gifted saleswomen Mary Kay had ever known enjoyed the drinks, not realizing the effect they would have on her, as she was unaccustomed to alcoholic beverages. This woman became so intoxicated that she acted in a way completely opposite to her usual dignified behavior. The next day, when she heard tales of what she had done, the saleswoman was so ashamed that she went home, quit the company, and never again pursued a selling career. Mary Kay learned from this experience, saying with regret, "I never want this company to be the cause of ruining anyone's promising career."

Mary Kay Inc. staff were admonished not to drink around the sales force as we were to set a good example. In 2004, the company held a

Leadership Conference in Nashville at the Gaylord Opryland Resort and Convention Center. This hotel is a self-contained biosphere with meeting rooms, shops, and restaurants, located outside of the city. My coworkers and I arrived on the staff bus from the airport and had no cars—we were stuck. Every restaurant in the establishment was filled with sales force members. I was with a group that wanted to relax after a particularly heavy work day; several of us wanted a glass of wine, but we knew we couldn't have the wine brought to us in wine glasses. It needed to be inconspicuous. We asked our waitress if she could bring each of us a glass of wine, perhaps in coffee cups. Instead, we got our wine in children's "sippy" cups!

Grand entrances were another big deal at Seminar, and Sue Z. became a company legend for developing ideas and selling Mary Kay on some truly outlandish introductions. She would go into Mary Kay's office and make an enthusiastic presentation. Afterwards, Mary Kay would tell me, "You will never believe what I just agreed to do."

Back in the 1960s, before regulations came into the picture, Sue Z. decided to climb up to the catwalk and have the stage manager hook her to a wire; she then "flew" down onto the stage. Another time, she borrowed a table from the kitchen, had it draped in white, reclined on it and had the kitchen staff surround her with fruit. Sue Z. then persuaded several tall bus boys to remove their shirts and carry her into the ballroom as she threw grapes into the audience.

One of Sue Z.'s most famous exploits was when she came in on an elephant. She had asked the special events director if she could have the aisles widened for this entrance, so he genuinely thought she was going to bring in a live elephant, but it turned out to be a life-sized artificial one.

The company planned extraordinary entrances for Mary Kay. Some of the most memorable included:

- a giant globe positioned at the back of the stage—the globe opened up, and out stepped Mary Kay;
- rising out of the floor via an elevating platform; unfortunately, the elevator jammed, and by the time the staff had rushed over to help her, Mary Kay had already crawled out onto the stage;
- entering from above in a hot air balloon lowered onto the stage; however, because Mary Kay's entrance was scheduled after an extravagant musical number, she had to be suspended above the stage for thirty minutes before her big moment.

For her most spectacular entrance, Mary Kay entered the arena in a Cinderella-like carriage pulled by two white stallions. She looked beautiful in her sparkling black evening gown, and the presentation was enchanting. Everyone later learned that there had been an incident with one of the horses before the start of the show. Mary Kay was seated in the carriage, interviewing with a local reporter, when suddenly, she heard a *whizzzz*, to which the reporter said, "I think one of your horses couldn't find the restroom."

When people ask me about my favorite Mary Kay memory, I tell them it involves the moments when Mary Kay made her entrances at any company event. When she stepped onstage, emotion and electricity permeated the room. There was never a dry eye in the arena. It didn't matter how many times I saw this happen: I always cried, too. The sales force loved their careers, and they cried because they were so grateful for the opportunity to keep their priorities in the proper order, achieve success, and experience personal growth. They showed their gratitude with applause and tears. They sat in the audience watching Mary Kay as I stood by the stage watching them, and I would always think, '*Look at the lives that Mary Kay has touched and enriched.*' Mine was one of those lives, too.

Sales force members who attended events where Mary Kay made her grand entrances always talk about the enormous electricity and feelings of energy and excitement that spread over the room. Love literally flowed between the sales force and Mary Kay.

In the 1970s, the company engaged popular motivators for the general assembly and famous entertainers for awards night. Mary Kay often invited noted Christian speakers, such as Dr. Robert Schuller, Zig Ziglar, Dr. Norman Vincent Peale, and Oral Roberts. As the sophistication of the top Sales Directors grew, however, Mary Kay realized that many of the women had become first-class motivational speakers themselves. The sales force preferred to hear success stories and tips from these outstanding women rather than hear from people outside the company. Today, the company primarily invites National Sales Directors and Top Sales Directors to speak at Seminar.

In the 1960s, entertainment at Seminar was provided by the staff and Sales Directors. They wrote and executed skits, and Mary Kay would always play her part. Sue Z. Vickers had a group called "The Vickeroos," in which she played the guitar and encouraged the audience to join in on the songs, including the ever-popular "Mary Kay Enthusiasm."

In the 1970s, the company featured well-known entertainers at awards nights, including Bobby Goldsboro, Tom Jones, Paul Anka, Glen Campbell, and B. J. Thomas. When the company booked the entertainers, the entertainers were always told to put on a clean show, but a few crossed the boundaries (none of those mentioned above were among this latter group). Mary Kay Inc. then created its own troupe of entertainers called the "Friends of Tyme," who performed spectacular numbers in a manner appropriate for a Mary Kay Inc. audience.

Mary Kay's speeches were full of her belief that God had His hands around Mary Kay Inc., and that He led and guided the company. The meetings always began with prayer, and a blessing was said before every meal—two traditions Mary Kay established that are still honored today.

For years, Seminar closed with a candlelight ceremony written by the Vice President of Sales. The lights in the auditorium were turned off, and one of the executives would light his or her candle, sharing what it represented, and then pass that light on to the next person in line. When the company debuted its first National Sales Directors, they were added to this ceremony. At the end of the ceremony, the participants would walk out into the audience and pass their lights on to others. As the number of Nationals grew, so did the number of candles. There finally came a time when the ceremony became too large and was discontinued, but I recall some of the sayings during the candlelight:

> "This light represents integrity . . . the integrity we practice in our daily lives."

> "This light represents love . . . the love of God, our country, and all mankind around us."

> "This light represents friendship . . . the warm friendship which we develop within the Mary Kay family."

> "This light represents devotion . . . the devotion to serving others cheerfully and diligently."

> "This light represents perseverance . . . the strength to say, 'I will not quit.'"

The most emotional Seminar I ever attended was in 1997; it was Mary Kay's last. This event took place a year and a half after her stroke, and she still had not regained her speech. However, she so greatly wanted to share with the sales force her love for them and her belief in their abilities. Mary Kay practiced her signature phrases—"You can do it," and "I love you"—over and over so she could share them with the sales force.

The top National Sales Director then read a letter to the audience that Mary Kay had written. In it, Mary Kay expressed her belief that God had entrusted her with the role of giving women an open-ended opportunity for success and that she was proud of the sales force for taking her dream and running with it. She also realized that there were many more lives that needed to be touched and that she expected the sales leaders and staff to continue building the "Mary Kay Way." The message ended with Mary Kay's iconic challenge: "You can do it!"

10

MARY KAY GOES GLOBAL

Who will not fear, O Lord, and glorify your name?
For you alone are holy. All nations will come and worship
you, for your righteous acts have been revealed.

REVELATION 15:4

The idea of giving women an open-ended opportunity
has catapulted countless thousands to achieve their dreams.
And now, women of many cultures are accepting our
opportunity in their own countries.

MARY KAY ASH[1]

When Mary Kay founded her company, she never dreamed it would grow beyond the Dallas area. As the company began to expand around the world, Mary Kay did not get excited about future profits. Her focus was on the lives that could be changed by offering women around the globe financial freedom and personal growth. When the presidents of Mary Kay subsidiaries came to Mary Kay's office to talk, she didn't want to hear facts and figures. She wanted to hear about the women who were building successful businesses and learn about the impact their careers had on their personal lives.

Mary Kay's international launch began in Australia in 1971, a decision that has surprised many who join the Mary Kay staff over the years as they wonder why she went all the way to Australia to open her first international market.

As always, she had her reasons. In 1966, an Australian gentleman who was visiting America contacted Mary Kay and Richard. He was studying American cosmetic companies and was so impressed with Mary Kay Cosmetics that he wanted to take the business to Australia. But Mary Kay and Richard were skeptical. Not only were they just starting to build the company themselves, but they could not imagine how they could manage a company halfway around the world.

When they politely declined, the man went back to Australia, founded a cosmetic company called Rachel York, and based it on the Mary Kay Cosmetics marketing plan. He would periodically contact Richard and give him the sales and production figures of his company. So, in August 1969, Mary Kay Cosmetics acquired Rachel York Pty., Ltd. as a subsidiary, and it became part of Mary Kay Inc. in 1971.

Mary Kay Inc. opened its second market in Canada, and Mary Kay was much more active in the Canadian launch because of its proximity to home. The company planned a cross-Canada tour, and they expected to host a series of guest nights in five cities, moving from east to west—Montreal, Toronto, Regina, Winnipeg, and Vancouver.

Mary Kay was excited to participate in her first Canadian tour. As she was getting ready for the first night in Montreal, the weather worsened, and the local television station warned viewers that they should not leave home unless they had an emergency. Mary Kay was amazed when she entered the venue for the event and saw over one hundred people there. The ballroom had massive glass windows, and outside was an absolute whiteout. That evening solidified Mary Kay's love for the Canadian people, and she called them the heartiest people she knew.

Anne Newbury participated in the first two Canadian guest nights held in Eastern Canada. Other United States Sales Directors dominated in Minneapolis and in the Northern Pacific regions, and Sales Directors from those areas crossed the border to join Mary Kay for the other three nights of the tour. After Mary Kay returned to Dallas, she called Anne to update her on the remaining three events and to express her concerns. Mary Kay told Anne that these new Mary Kay Beauty Consultants needed training, and she wanted them to be trained not only in the basics of the Mary Kay business but also in the company philosophies. Mary Kay asked Anne if she would return to Canada and hold training meetings, which Anne was most willing to do. Under the Mary Kay Go-Give Program, Anne didn't receive any personal remuneration for this training, but Anne felt that her business would thrive if she helped others.

This philosophy of women helping women with no regard to their personal compensation is one aspect of the Mary Kay marketing plan that others outside the company find hard to understand. But Mary Kay has proven that this philosophy works. Being asked by Mary Kay Inc. to speak or train is looked upon as a privilege, and women give of their time from their hearts and out of their love for others. Mary Kay taught that "all you send into the lives of others comes back into your own." This principle has been proven countless times by women who have helped others unselfishly, only to find that their careers flourished because of their actions.

After the initial Canadian opening, the company planned a public relations tour where Mary Kay would participate in radio, television, and newspaper interviews. The company wanted to showcase a pink Cadillac as they moved across the country, so they asked Anne if she would be Mary Kay's chauffeur. The launch started with a newspaper interview in Mary Kay's hotel suite; Anne then picked up Mary Kay and Mel at their hotel to drive them to Mary Kay's interviews. The public relations agent maintained the schedule and rode in the front seat with Anne. When the group got stuck in a traffic jam, the agent announced that they would have to skip the next interview.

Anne looked in her rearview mirror and could see that Mary Kay was distressed. Cell phones were unheard of at this time, so there was no way to call and let the show know of the change of plans. Anne knew Mary Kay did not want the interviewers to think that she had stood them up, so she asked Mary Kay, "Do I have your permission to do whatever I have to do to get us there?" "Absolutely," Mary Kay responded. Anne saw an opening ahead of them, so she turned the car onto the sidewalk and drove down an alley that led to another street that was not busy. They arrived at the radio station on time. As Mary Kay exited the car, she leaned toward Anne and said, "Honey, you drive just like I do. Keep it up."

In 1980, Mary Kay Inc. opened in Argentina. In the early 1980s, Mary Kay and some of the other executives began taking Spanish lessons because they wanted to communicate with the Latina sales force in their language, both in the United States and Argentina. They signed up for Spanish lessons at the Berlitz Language Center in Dallas where National Sales Director Emeritus Gladys Reyes had recently joined as a staff member.[2]

Gladys also had another job as a translator. Because she had small children, Gladys only worked part-time for these two different companies. The translating company called Gladys and begged her to take an assignment that required her attendance every day for one week. After making childcare arrangements with her husband, Gladys arrived at the address for the job, only to find that it was the Mary Kay headquarters.

As Gladys entered the building, she heard people in an auditorium clapping and laughing. When she inquired in the human relations department about where to report, she was pointed to the auditorium. In attendance were two hundred women, fourteen of whom spoke

Spanish. Gladys and her group were seated at a table at the back of the auditorium with no translation equipment. Mary Kay was introduced, and everyone began singing, clapping, and crying. Gladys thought, "If this woman is loved by so many people, this must be a special company." By the end of the week, Gladys was singing, clapping, and crying with everyone else. The women cried because their lives had been changed, and Gladys cried with them. The last day of the week ended with a candlelight ceremony. As she was leaving, Gladys expressed her interest in translating for Mary Kay Inc. whenever they needed anyone, and she became the company's permanent Spanish translator.

One day, Mary Kay asked Gladys, "Why should I go to the school when you can just teach me here?" For six months, Gladys came to Mary Kay's office and gave her lessons. Mary Kay saw potential in Gladys and encouraged her to become a Mary Kay Beauty Consultant many times. When Gladys told Mary Kay that she was too shy to sell, Mary Kay said "Don't say shy; say introverted." She explained to Gladys that women didn't have to change when they joined Mary Kay Inc. Gladys decided to join to show everyone at the company that she couldn't sell just so they would quit asking. Instead, she built a successful business.

By 1988, when Mary Kay Inc. opened in Mexico, Gladys's unit had grown to the level of earning a pink Cadillac, and Mary Kay asked her to help with the Mexico opening. Gladys held a training class for the first sales force members in Mexico. As Gladys remembers this event, "There were nine Beauty Consultants who had formerly been with other cosmetic companies. Eight of these became National Sales Directors. The more I talked about the philosophies, the more they loved the idea of a company where they would not have to sacrifice their faith and their families for success. Mary Kay's philosophies are perfect for the Latin woman. Family and faith are so very important to them. I knew Mary Kay Mexico would embrace this philosophy."

Gladys also attended the grand opening of Mary Kay Inc. Mexico in Monterrey with Mary Kay. As always, Mary Kay's charisma drew people to her. Nervous women inquired of Gladys, "When I meet her, what should I say?" However, the moment they saw Mary Kay, they would start crying, unable to say a thing.

Mary Kay decided to give her speech in Spanish. After she wrote it, she asked Gladys to translate it. They then practiced and practiced and practiced. Mary Kay wanted the Mexican sales force to know how important they were to her.

Mary Kay was not able to visit every international market the company opened, but she did make several trips to the subsidiary in Germany.[3] She was there shortly after the fall of the Berlin Wall. One of Mary Kay's favorite stories happened at a Mary Kay Inc. meeting she attended there. Sales force members came across the stage, and when one of them got to the microphone, she said, "First we get freedom; and now we get Mary Kay!" Of course, Mary Kay was thrilled.

Several years ago, I was at a dinner with some members of the German sales force who were visiting Dallas for Seminar. When I told them about Mary Kay's love for Seminar and about her often repeating the Berlin Wall story, I was surprised to learn that the woman who made the freedom and Mary Kay statement was seated at my table. Ursel Ebert, who had built her Mary Kay business to the level of National Sales Director, had grown up in a small village in former East Germany called Thuringia. When she attended her first Mary Kay Inc. meeting, Ursel was impressed with Mary Kay's dreams for women as well as her philosophies, including building a business by the Golden Rule.

After Ursel joined the company, she heard that Mary Kay Ash was coming to Germany and wanted to meet her. At that Seminar in Munich, Ursel was impressed by Mary Kay's charisma and vision. She realized that Mary Kay's words truly came from her heart. Mary Kay encouraged Ursel, and she became convinced that "Mary Kay offers women a unique opportunity." Following her own dream, Ursel became the third Sales Director in Germany and then the first National Sales Director in the country, sharing her career not only with West German women but also with those who had lived under Communist rule in East Germany.

Mary Kay Inc. continued its foreign expansion, and Mary Kay's excitement grew as she realized that the company was touching the lives of women all over the world. By 1995, Mary Kay products were sold in over twenty-five countries on five continents, including Russia and China. One day, Mary Kay remarked to me, "With all of our different markets, every minute of every single day, somewhere in the world, a Mary Kay skin care class is being held."

One of the goals of the company's culture committee—on which I was proud to serve for several years—is to help spread the Mary Kay culture around the world in markets where Mary Kay Inc. exists. The company has found that the most successful subsidiaries are those that successfully incorporate Mary Kay Inc. ideals into their interactions between the staff and the sales force.

Mary Kay employees were once asked to pick a favorite Mary Kay saying and post it on their doors, along with a message of its importance. I chose, "All you send into the lives of others comes back into your own." As my reasoning for its selection, I wrote, "This quote is my favorite because Mary Kay built this company on the Golden Rule and on giving into the lives of others. Out of these principles came the Go-Give spirit, Golden Rule service, and The Mary Kay Foundation. Mary Kay not only set an example of giving, which certainly bore fruit in her life, but she also taught others to give. Around the world, independent sales force members and Mary Kay employees have joined Mary Kay in giving back to the lives of their fellow associates and their communities. So much good is being done around the world in the name of Mary Kay because she lived her life by this principle—from helping domestic violence victims in countries like Canada, Mexico, and the United States to supporting children's causes in Portugal, Poland, China, Germany, and Russia. This makes me so proud to be a part of Mary Kay Inc."

No matter what the local customs may be, all people want to be treated the way Mary Kay taught—with the Golden Rule philosophy and as if they are the most important person in the room. The Golden Rule is taught in every major religion; it's just worded a little differently.[4]

Christianity	"So whatever you wish that others would do to you, do also to them, for this is the Law and the Prophets."—Matthew 7:12
Confucianism	"Do not do to others what you would not like yourself. Then there will be no resentment against you, either in the family or in the state."—Analects 12:2
Judaism	"What is hateful to you, do not do to your fellowman. This is the entire Law; all the rest is commentary."—Talmud, Shabbat 3id
Buddhism	"Hurt not others in ways that you yourself would find hurtful."—UdanaVarga 5.18
Hinduism	"This is the sum of duty; do naught unto others what you would not have them do unto you."—Mahabharata 5.1517
Islam	"No one of you is a believer until he desires for his brother that which he desires for himself."—Sunnah

11

MARY KAY THE CHRISTIAN

The fear of the Lord leads to life, and whoever has it rests satisfied; he will not be visited by harm.

PROVERBS 19:23

Our belief in God should never be checked at the door when we punch a time clock. Faith is a 24-hour-a-day commitment. Many women have made the mistake of changing their beliefs to accommodate their work; it must be the other way around. No circumstance is so unusual that it demands a double standard or separates us from our faith.

MARY KAY ASH[1]

Mary Kay's relationship with God was at the core of her company. As she states in *You Can Have It All*, "God was my first priority early in my career when I was struggling to make ends meet; through the failures and successes I have experienced since then, my faith has remained unshaken."[2] Her life philosophy was, "God first, family second, and career third." Company meetings and meals opened with prayer. Mary Kay took God as her partner, and she always gave Him the credit for any success she might have.

Mary Kay wanted her company to not only help women financially, but also emotionally and spiritually. She wove her faith into her speeches, her correspondence, and her actions. Acknowledging God ultimately made a big difference in the company's success.

Mary Kay's lifelong prayer was that God would use her. He used her to open opportunities for women in the 1960s, and He used her to open doors for women to see His light through her example and teachings. Because of Mary Kay's faith, the sales force developed a strong belief that God would provide and that difficulties could be overcome.

During the years I worked for her, I was always inspired by the many beautiful letters Mary Kay received from sales force members and others that expressed how her commitment to putting God first had influenced their lives. People shared with Mary Kay how they had either come to know Christ, had recommitted their lives to Him, or had developed a deeper relationship with Him because of her encouragement to put Him first.

On one of *The 700 Club* programs on which Mary Kay appeared, co-host Ben Kinchlow interviewed members of the audience, many of whom were Mary Kay sales force members. They echoed the sentiments of so many whose lives have been changed because of the influence of Mary Kay Ash.

When Virginia Beach Sales Director Barbara Sawyer was asked what a Mary Kay career had done for her, she answered that it had brought her closer to God, adding, "We have a sisterhood, and we are very close to Mary Kay. She truly is our mother . . . She wants us to reach our fullest potential and make as much money as we want to." Susan Smith from Portsmouth, Virginia, shared with the audience that the Mary Kay opportunity showed her that "there are people out there who love God and love us, and we can be beautiful on the outside as well as on the inside."[3]

These testimonies brought Mary Kay more joy than growing sales numbers. She was not interested in financial figures; she was interested in changing lives. To her, these were the company's real successes.

Mickey Ivey, whose husband was a pastor, related that God used her more as a Mary Kay businesswoman than he did as a pastor's wife. Women were intimidated by her role as a pastor's wife, but as a businesswoman, they felt a connection. "I never tried to evangelize. I just expressed Mary Kay's principles, and God opened doors for me. I was part of a company that respected who I was and how I lived and gave me the freedom to live that way."

Mickey would tell people that Mary Kay Inc. asked the sales force to do something no other company had asked: to keep God first, family second, and career third. Mickey believed that women were not meant to live their lives in boxes, hopping from Christian to mother to career woman. Rather, they could "roll their lives into one ball" as they lived their faith twenty-four hours a day, seven days a week. Mary Kay taught Mickey that "a woman doesn't have to separate all the areas in her life. My Mary Kay career blended with my Christianity, and my Christianity blended with my career."

Church was important to Mary Kay, so she was an active member of a local church. National Sales Director Jill Moore, Mickey's daughter, attended the same church as Mary Kay and recalls seeing her sitting on the front row every Sunday with Zig Ziglar's wife, Jean.[4] "While some people say they go to church, their attendance is sporadic," Jill noted. "Mary Kay was there every Sunday, always in the same spot."

One of the most dramatic stories of how God used Mary Kay to change lives is that of Kathy Helou. Kathy won a Mary Kay skin care set on *The Price is Right*—a moment that completely changed her life. As Kathy recalls, "I look back and see that God's plan for me was to win that skin care system instead of the Mazda."

As a child, Kathy rode to church on Sundays in a church bus, but she never really understood the good news Jesus preached. After joining Mary Kay Inc., Kathy met Sue Uibel, whose husband was a music minister at the local Baptist church. Kathy saw something in the Uibels she knew she didn't have. Although she couldn't put a label on it, she loved being around them.

Kathy's Mary Kay Inc. career began to soar, and others were interested in her success story. Mary Kay called Kathy to ask if she would speak at an upcoming Leadership Conference. Kathy was so scared by the idea of speaking before a large audience that Mary Kay sensed it through the phone. She asked Kathy, "May I ask you something? Do you know who Jesus is?" Kathy told her that she had been to church, but Mary Kay persisted, "But do you *know* Him?" When Kathy asked what she meant, Mary Kay shared Jesus with her.[5]

After Kathy's Leadership Conference speech, Pam Kelly, a Sales Director whom Kathy did not know, sent her a Bible. In a note to Kathy, she wrote, "After hearing you speak, I know God is going to use you in a mighty way." Kathy started reading that Bible, and her life changed. These three incidents—meeting the Uibels, hearing the good news of Jesus from Mary Kay, and receiving the Bible from Pam—all happened within Kathy's first year with Mary Kay Inc.

God also had plans for Kathy's children. "God not only changed my life through Mary Kay, but He also changed generations. I was raised by parents who did not know the Lord. I raised my children differently. I began reading the Bible to them. Now my grandchildren are being raised the same way."

Over the years, God has raised up dynamic prayer warriors in Mary Kay Inc. In August 2018, I received a video of Executive Senior National Sales Director Stacy James leading a powerful prayer backstage at Seminar.[6] As a new National Sales Director attending her first Summit, Stacy was so impressed with Mary Kay's opening the meeting in prayer, the sincerity of her prayer, and the way that she wove lessons for all of them into her heartfelt words. Stacy experienced a depth and length of prayer to which she had never been exposed.

When Stacy started with Mary Kay Inc., she believed in God, but she did not have a personal relationship with the Lord. Through the company, she was exposed to women who knew God intimately, and she wanted what they had. Stacy felt that their conversations were anointed, and that these women had learned to live their faith from Mary Kay. They had incorporated into their own careers Mary Kay's philosophies and principles—generosity, people helping people, and selflessness instead of selfishness. These women operated their businesses with a belief in God as their foundation, and they helped lead Stacy to Christ.

Stacy grew up in a positive family. She had read lots of popular books on the concept of being positive, but until she accepted Jesus, she didn't understand that these principles grew out of Biblical teachings. Stacy saw that the desire to help other people was at the very core of everything Mary Kay did. Mary Kay built a company on the philosophy that a leader must help others to become successful.

Stacy was not only impressed with Mary Kay's commitment to corporate prayer, but she also saw Mary Kay pray personally for those in need of comfort. At one of the leadership meetings that Stacy attended, she noticed Mary Kay approach a Sales Director backstage and lead her to a private area. Stacy watched as Mary Kay hugged this woman and prayed for her. She later learned that the Sales Director's husband, who was in the military, had been killed. Mary Kay wanted to be the one to tell this woman of the tragic news. She truly felt the Sales Directors were her Mary Kay daughters, and she took the responsibility to share the unthinkable.

Elite Executive National Sales Director Jan Harris became Stacy's mentor. Before they went into an appointment to present the marketing plan, Stacy remembers Jan praying, "If this is not for her, help us to be gracious and understand that. If this *is* for her, help her to open her heart and have us deliver what she needs to hear." Jan's attitude changed Stacy's own presentation and how she viewed her appointments.

Stacy ultimately found that prayer is a big part of many sales force leaders' lives. Before the major events begin, the National Sales Directors meet and pray over the event from start to finish. They have learned the importance of prayer through the National Sales Director Summits, where they pray not only at the beginning but also together in small groups throughout the event. They pray for the company's direction and that they will be Mary Kay's light and torch, keeping her principles and the culture alive.

Another notable Mary Kay Inc. prayer warrior is National Sales Director Emeritus Kirk Gillespie.[7] Kirk was brought up in a church with sound doctrine, but she never understood what a personal relationship with the Lord looked like. In college, she attended a rally led by Josh McDowell; this event marked a turning point in her relationship with God. When she started her Mary Kay career, Kirk grew in her walk with the Lord. Although Mary Kay never preached, Kirk saw that Mary Kay and the other women she met through the company had a joy that she wanted. "Mary Kay lived her faith so beautifully," Kirk says. "One of my favorite memories was when PETA picketed outside of the Mary Kay manufacturing building because, like most cosmetic companies at that time, the products were tested on animals.[8] It was a hot, Texas summer day, and Mary Kay took pink lemonade to the protesters. She truly lived by the Golden Rule."

Kirk decided that one way she could give back to the company was through prayer, so she started a prayer group of National Sales Directors from around the country. They hold a weekly conference call to pray for each other, people they know, the company, and issues that they feel are important. As women have come in and out of this prayer group, Kirk has watched them grow spiritually. Others have heard about what they are doing and have asked to join. Kirk has found that six to eight members make up an ideal prayer group. Since her group is full, Kirk encourages other sales force members to start their own prayer circles, hoping that her group inspires "prayer pockets" all over the nation.

Kathy Helou remembers Mary Kay praying for her specifically when she needed it. Kathy was eight months pregnant when she travelled to China with the top Sales Directors, Mary Kay, and key staff members as part of a reward for her achievements during the past year. Today, Kathy is amazed that her doctors even let her travel, but none of them said anything to make her think that taking an international trip at eight months along might not be a wise idea. Because she was the top Sales Director, Kathy had the privilege of sitting next to Mary Kay at dinner one night. The food they were served was so strange to her, and she could not eat it. Kathy had some crackers in her purse, and Mary Kay noticed her nibbling on those.

Since Mary Kay had trouble eating the food as well, she leaned over and asked Kathy, "Aren't you going to share those with me?" Kathy told Mary Kay that she wasn't ungrateful; she just couldn't get past some of the smells. After the meal, a cake with flaming candles was delivered to their table in celebration of one of the Sales Director's birthday. Mary Kay turned to Kathy and said, "Here's something we can eat!" She received the first piece, and then gestured to Kathy and said, "My friend over here needs the second piece."

After dinner, Kathy was in her room getting ready for bed when she heard a knock at the door. She opened the door, and there stood Mary Kay. She walked in and said, "I just wanted to see how you are doing and pray for you. I know you are not doing well." Mary Kay prayed that everything would go well with Kathy's pregnancy, that she would not get sick and would make it through the trip, and that she would trust God with her future. After the prayer, Mary Kay noticed that Kathy had been writing her newsletter for her unit. She asked if she could make a video for Kathy's group. With Kathy—in her pajamas—beside her, Mary Kay picked up the newsletter and called out the names of those being recognized. She congratulated their accomplishments and even set goals for others to reach the next level.

Because of Mary Kay's commitment to the Lord, her presence drew many Christians to the company, and she was always an encouragement to them. In one of the company newsletters, Terry Bearden, a member of the Mary Kay Manufacturing Management Team, shared a story of the time he was asked to pray at a Manufacturing Safety Recognition luncheon. After hearing his blessing, Mary Kay approached him and asked if she could go through the serving line with him. She expressed her appreciation for his prayer, and they talked about their shared faith. Later that year, Mary Kay invited Terry to give the prayer at the employee Christmas dinner party.

In the mid-1980s, Wilda DeKerlegand needed advice and direction. The economy was in a slump, and so was her business. Although she was the number one Sales Director, Wilda felt like she was working in quicksand. Other sales force members felt the same way. Banks weren't giving loans to women wanting to start their Mary Kay businesses, even banks with whom Wilda had done business for a long time. Not knowing what to do, Wilda booked an appointment with Mary Kay in Dallas and shared with her the economic climate she faced.

When Wilda started to cry, Mary Kay rose from her chair and told Wilda to stand up and lift her skirt above her knees. "I see a little blood and a few scratches," Mary Kay said observantly. Then Mary Kay lifted her own skirt above her knees and said, "Look at these knees. Look at all the blood that's been there, look at the gashes. But you know what, here I am. I made it, and you certainly can, too. Let's pray." She prayed, "Lord, when we know that we are not in control, we know the One who is in control." They prayed about Wilda's business and for the leaders and success of the company.

As Mary Kay Inc. has grown and the Mary Kay opportunity has opened to women of all faiths in many different countries, the company asked that the Sales Directors and National Sales Directors not end their prayers in Jesus's name at corporate events. The first time Mary Kay was asked to not close her prayer in Jesus's name, she complied. The next time I saw her, she was miserable. "I feel like such a hypocrite," she told me. "I will never do that again. I just can't pray without ending with, 'in Jesus's name.'" Many in the company also feel this dilemma. Once, when Nan Stroud was scheduled to give the invocation at one of the earliest Seminars, she asked Mary Kay, "How should I close my prayer?" Knowing Nan's deep faith, Mary Kay answered without hesitation, "In Jesus's name, of course. How would you pray any other way?"

While I understand the company's position, I also knew Mary Kay's heart. She started this company so women could keep God first in their lives with *their* God. Many Christian sales force members feel compromised when they are asked to pray at company-sponsored events, but they honor the company's wishes. At the same time, they appreciate that they can express their love for Jesus in non-threatening ways at the meetings they organize and lead. Many retreats have offered optional Sunday morning services for the attending sales force members, where I and others have been pleased to share our testimonies of Mary Kay's influence in our lives.

Mary Kay's decision to bring prayer into Mary Kay Inc. events always resulted in others criticizing her, but she remained adamant that her company open its meetings and its meals with a prayer to God. Even in the 1970s, some people questioned Mary Kay's stance on prayer, but Mary Kay always invited her pastor to open Seminar in prayer. At an early National Sales Directors meeting, several women urged Mary Kay not to open with prayer; if she did, she should invite a leader from another religion to lead the invocation. Mickey Ivey said that Mary Kay sat there very calmly during this discussion. Mickey then spoke up, saying, "Mary Kay's God is Jesus Christ, not *a* god." At that point, Mary Kay interjected, "Enough said," and the meeting continued.

Sarah Larr was beginning her career in entertainment when she first met Mary Kay in 1973. Mary Kay had listened to Sarah's singing group and asked them to perform at that year's Seminar. When Mary Kay inquired about what name she should use when presenting Sarah's group, Sarah said, "Friends." Mary Kay named them, "The Friends of Tyme."

Backstage, Mary Kay always passed through the entertainers' dressing room on her way to hair and makeup, and she would stop and pray with the group before Seminar started. As Sarah's troupe expanded and experienced turnover in personnel, she would hire new members. At the end of the auditions, after making her selections, Sarah would call the newest members together and tell them about the group's tradition of prayer and about Mary Kay's God first, family second, and career third philosophy. If someone didn't feel comfortable with this philosophy, she wanted to give that person the opportunity to decline the position. However, she never had one singer or dancer complain.

BEYOND BORDERS

Mary Kay's Christian impact reached beyond the borders of the United States. Mary Kay truly wanted others to see Jesus in her. She often said, "We may be the only Bible that some people might ever read." She knew that every word she spoke and everything she did was watched and, many times, emulated by those around her.

Birgit Johnson, the number one National Sales Director in Germany, remembers the very first time she heard these words. In 1987, when she debuted as the first German Sales Director, she was presented with her first Sales Director check onstage at that year's Seminar. There, Mary Kay said to her, "Birgit, you will be the only Bible that some people might ever read, so always walk the straight way." Intrigued by those words, Birgit picked up the Bible in her hotel room that night and started reading it. She continued reading the Bible daily, and it changed her life as she came to know God and His purpose for her life.

Birgit's career blossomed in Germany. She became the first car winner, the first Senior National Sales Director, and the first Inner Circle National Sales Director. She has held the title of number one National Sales Director in Germany since she gained that title in 1994. Mary Kay planted a seed of faith in Birgit's life when she was in the United States, and she then built a successful career with a Christian foundation in Germany. Birgit told me, "I will be forever thankful. I promised Mary Kay Ash that I would pass it on. And I am."

Mary Kay also had an influence on Christianity in China. After her stroke, Mary Kay received a letter from a woman who had taught English in China for thirteen years. She and her daughter were driving in Beijing when she saw a billboard advertising Mary Kay Cosmetics. When she expressed her surprise at the billboard, her daughter related that some Beauty Consultants in China had started attending her church. They were impressed with the company's philosophy of God first, family second, and career third, and they wanted to learn more about Mary Kay's God.

As the Mary Kay international markets expanded, National Sales Directors and Sales Directors in many countries were eager to know about Mary Kay the woman. Mary Kay Inc. often sent some of the pioneer National Sales Directors from the United States to places around the world to teach classes and to share stories of Mary Kay.

Because some corporate executives were concerned about the effect that Mary Kay's God-first philosophy would have upon non-Christian markets, they cautioned the pioneers to refrain from talking about their personal religious beliefs in their teachings. For so many of these women, however, their Mary Kay successes were contingent on a belief in God and how they had seen Him work in their careers.

Sue Kirkpatrick was asked to mentor the Latin American Sales Directors on a Baltic cruise and was assigned to teach two classes. Her husband Kirk had written a poem—called "Lord, I Need to Be a Winner"—that Mary Kay liked and had printed in company publications; she also used it to close one of her speeches.[9] When Sue recited this poem, the English-speaking Latin American National Sales Directors started reciting it with her in Spanish. These words had touched those in the Latin American countries, and many of them used the poem to inspire others.

At a dinner that Sue attended for the newest international Nationals, she honored the corporate request to refrain from speaking about her personal relationship with God. However, she noticed that one of the Chinese National Sales Directors wore a cross necklace. When someone asked the woman if she was a Christian, she said that she wasn't; she had simply bought the necklace because she thought it was pretty. The woman's interpreter was a Christian, and she began asking him questions about Christianity. At the end of the week, she attended the interpreter's church with him and was baptized.

Kathy Helou remembers when two overseas Mary Kay Inc. subsidiaries asked her to speak to their sales force; they requested she not use any references to God. Kathy apologized but declined the invitation, saying that she would not be able to come because the Lord was part of her Mary Kay experience. As the first Sales Director to break the two-million-dollar unit sales barrier and one of the top National Sales Directors in the United States, the subsidiaries really wanted her expertise, so they withdrew their request that Kathy make no mention of her faith. Kathy agreed to speak to their sales forces, and she shared how God had worked in her life through Mary Kay Inc. She quoted Jeremiah 29:11: "For I know the plans I have for you, declares the LORD, plans for welfare and not for evil, to give you a future and a hope."

After Kathy's speech, the sales force members lined up to speak with her and consistently asked her about that verse. When she returned to the United States, she received emails from the sales force members in these two countries with more questions about her faith, stating that they wanted to buy Bibles. When Mary Kay heard stories like Kathy's, she would say that her founding Mary Kay Inc. was divinely orchestrated.

My Answered Prayers

Like so many others at Mary Kay Inc., during my years at the company, I experienced the power of prayer and how God answers them—sometimes in ways you expect, and sometimes in ways that you do not. There are those little prayers one sends heavenward, such as asking for help in finding one's car keys. Then there are those vitally important prayers which God answers in personal, powerful, and significant ways. When He does, I am always surprised. I then stop and think, "Why am I surprised? God has promised to answer the prayers of His children." I have learned that God hears me, Jennifer Susan Bickel Cook, and that an all-powerful God cares about imperfect me. God is the Creator of the universe, and He still hears me when I pray. What an awesome thought!

I would be the first to admit, however, there have been times when it has been difficult to pray, and other times when I felt that God did not hear my prayers. I do not claim to be a prayer warrior, a mighty intercessor who prays night and day. I have had periods of regular prayer and dry spells of erratic prayer, but I do know the power of prayer. During my prayer life, some answers have been instantaneous; others have taken months. My spiritual walk is full of periods of growth followed by periods of stagnation.

During my career at Mary Kay, I was a working mother facing the challenges that so many women face today: trying to balance a busy career with being a wife, mother, and member of a religious community. I often felt like I had little alone time for prayer and meditation. But twice in my life, I prayed what I call a "God owns the cattle on a thousand hills" prayer. His amazing answers to these two requests for divine help are a testimony to how God used Mary Kay in my life.

The first time that I prayed the "cattle on a thousand hills" prayer was when my daughter Mary Elizabeth was a junior in high school. In anticipation of her graduation, she and I had started visiting universities; she had chosen two in Oklahoma, the University of Oklahoma and the University of Tulsa. The University of Tulsa is a private university and therefore the more expensive of the two. However, as soon as we stepped on that campus, I had the feeling that God wanted Mary Elizabeth to go to the University of Tulsa. It offered all that she wanted in a university, and she was so excited.

While we were in the decision-making process, the "worry" part of me took over. How could I afford this? Would Mary Elizabeth be having a great time in college while we were all at home eating beans and wieners? I became obsessed with worry until I realized that I needed to pray about this concern. One night, I got on my knees and prayed the "cattle on a thousand hills" prayer, ending with, "If Mary Elizabeth is to go to the University of Tulsa, I know you can supply the funds out of your abundant riches." The *very next day*, Mary Kay's bookkeeper came to see me (this was after Mary Kay's stroke, when she was unable to come into the office). She informed me that Mary

Kay had given me a tax-free gift of $25,000. I was stunned. I had prayed for help just the night before, and the next day God delivered. Mary Kay was His vehicle. I couldn't wait to see Mary Kay, not only to thank her, but also to tell her how God had miraculously used her to answer an urgent prayer.

The second time I used the "cattle on a thousand hills" prayer involved my work as Director of The Mary Kay Foundation. I was responsible for raising money for the MK5K, an annual race benefitting the eradication of women's cancers and the elimination of violence against women. After calling our sponsors one year, I learned that one of our $10,000 partners would not be participating in the MK5K effort. I also learned that several other sponsors would not be donating, and at that point, I grew concerned. I decided to pray. I got down on my knees and told God that I didn't know how new sponsors would materialize, but I knew that He could provide the money because He owns the cattle on a thousand hills. The *very next day*, one of our generous sponsors called to say that they were increasing their donation from $5,000 to $10,000. A few days later, their parent company also wanted to donate $10,000.

God then continued to open His storehouse of funds. A week before the MK5K, a major insurance company called regarding a $5,000 donation. A local agent had reached a milestone sales volume goal, and his company was giving $5,000 in his name to the charity of his choice. One of his office members, whose daughter worked at Mary Kay, was struggling with cancer. Her daughter was part of an MK5K team and was raising money for that team. The local agent made the decision to support his office member and her daughter, and $5,000 was added to the daughter's team total. Thanks to prayer, God supplied an additional $20,000 for the MK5K!

I also had an answered prayer in 2005 when my father was in the last days of his life. My mother was always a woman of faith. Although my father was a decent, honest, and successful businessman who loved his wife and family, he had a short temper and often cursed and raged. He came from a godly heritage, though, and both of my fraternal grandparents were deeply religious. My grandfather had died many years before my grandmother, who, when she was in her nineties, was still serving the Lord by helping to care for an invalid who lived nearby. My sister Bonny and I always say that we want our twilight years to be like Grandmother Bickel's, surrounded by believers and doing the Lord's work right until the end.

As my Dad's last days were imminent, I was uncertain of his salvation and had an urgent need to know that he would be in Heaven. At that time, my church had distributed a book that combined the four gospels in chronological order, and I asked Dad if he would like me to read it to him. He agreed, and I visited every day to read until he was tired. Some days it wasn't the right time to read, but I was not discouraged. God had impressed on me that my father would not pass away until we finished the book. After reading the last page, I was able to talk to Dad about salvation, and he told me that he believed. It was another answered prayer, and I felt peace.

12

MY STORY

The heart of man plans his way,
but the LORD *establishes his steps.*

PROVERBS 16:9

Most successful people will tell you: "If it were not for
the help of other people, I wouldn't be where I am today."
I believe that everybody who accomplishes something
great has had help from someone. Somebody, somewhere,
provided a spark of inspiration, offered a challenge,
or held out a hand along the way.

MARY KAY ASH[1]

When I walked through the doors of Mary Kay Cosmetics in 1971, I began a journey that would last forty-five years. At that point in time, the company was very young, and so was I—I was nineteen. I had just completed two years at the University of Texas at Arlington and was already married. My parents told me that they would continue to pay my tuition, but that my living expenses were my own.

In need of a summer job, I signed on with a temporary agency that sent me to Mary Kay Cosmetics because the Vice President of Administration needed someone to fill in as his secretary until he found a replacement. His secretary had moved to California, where she became a Mary Kay Independent Beauty Consultant and later became one of the top saleswomen in the Mary Kay business, a National Sales Director. Her decision to leave turned out to be advantageous for the both of us.

For the next two years, I continued working my way through college at Mary Kay Cosmetics, putting in extra hours during the summers and arranging my schedule during the school year so I could work on Mondays, Wednesdays, and Fridays while taking courses on Tuesdays and Thursdays. These were rough financial years. My husband and I were on a tight budget, and sometimes we barely had any money. We would go to construction sites and pick up glass Coke bottles, recyclable for a dime, take them to the grocery store, and cash them in to buy bread. We never once thought of borrowing money because that just wasn't something people did back then. On one occasion, all we had in the house was a box of macaroni and cheese and some baloney, so I got the great idea of making a baloney casserole. It was horrible!

I remember well the time when I wrecked my old, second-hand car after I started working at Mary Kay Cosmetics. Since I could only afford liability and not collision insurance, a new, black, side-panel was put on my white vehicle, but I didn't have the money to get it painted to match my car. Imagine my embarrassment when I had to give a ride to Dick Bartlett, who was at that time the President of Mary Kay Cosmetics, from the convention center to a local hotel during Seminar. He just laughed, trying to put me at ease by telling me he had driven some real rattletraps when he was working his way through college, too.

Those hard times taught me the value of balancing my checkbook with the little finances we had, and I passed the lessons I learned about money management on to my children. Fortunately, my daughter Mary Elizabeth and my son Stephen graduated from college debt free. Mary Elizabeth built a career in education, obtaining her masters and doctorate degrees and moving into administration. Stephen received a Bachelor of Science degree in nutrition from Oklahoma State University and eventually obtained an R.N. at Stephen F. Austin University in Nacogdoches, Texas, to help him achieve his goal of becoming a wellness coordinator.

During my early years at Mary Kay Inc., though, I had to be content with what I had while working for a brighter future. In 1974, I finally graduated with a major in English and a minor in French, with enough educational courses to obtain my teaching certificate. The Irving Independent School District—where I had attended high school—had given me a scholarship toward my teaching degree, so I felt obligated to apply for a job with them, but secretly hoped my application would be denied. I absolutely loved my job at Mary Kay Cosmetics and wanted to stay with the company. As luck had it, there was a glut within the teaching market at the time, and no job was available.

This seemingly negative situation on the teaching front was truly providential. Although I did not realize it at the time, God was leading me towards His chosen career for my life. Mary Kay needed someone with my skill set in communication, and within a few months, she appointed me as her Executive Secretary. Given my youth and inexperience, I couldn't help but wonder what Mary Kay was thinking! But, as I was to learn, Mary Kay could see the potential in people, and she must have seen something in me.

Many important events in my personal life took place during my forty-five years at Mary Kay Inc. In 1978, my daughter Mary Elizabeth was born, and then, in 1983, my life was sadly impacted by divorce. In 1985, I married Rodney Cook, and we had two sons, Christopher in 1985 and Stephen in 1989. Mary Kay was totally supportive through all these developments. I will never forget when my daughter was four years old and had somehow gotten into and ingested medicine at her daycare facility. When the daycare called to inform me that they had sent her to the hospital, I was almost paralyzed with fear. As soon as Mary Kay learned what had happened, she got me out the door quickly. "You've got to leave now! Put down what you are doing," she ordered me, rousing me from my state of shock.

The most life-transforming event during my years with Mary Kay, however, was coming to know the Lord. As Mary Kay's Executive Secretary, I couldn't help but observe that her faith was a big part of her life. She gave God the credit for her success, encouraged others to put Him first in their lives, and talked about Him as if she knew Him personally.

Although I was raised in the Methodist church, religion wasn't important to me. I just wasn't interested, perhaps because the church our family attended had some teachings that I later discovered to be erroneous. My Sunday School teacher convinced me that the feedings of the five thousand and later of the four thousand weren't miracles, but that Jesus simply encouraged others to share their food and that that was how everyone was fed. She failed to mention the part where twelve baskets and seven baskets of broken pieces were taken up after everyone had eaten their fill. There was no acknowledgement of a miracle-performing Savior who had died for my sins.

My parents took me to church regularly, and my grandmother sent me issues of *Decision* magazine, which I discarded.[2] After my confirmation ceremony at the age of twelve, my mother told me that she didn't feel I should have participated because I didn't really understand what it meant to be a Christian. I couldn't comprehend what she was talking about.

Truth be told, I didn't even know what sin was. When I was once at the Texas State Fair, evangelists once stopped me and started talking about the Bible. They quoted from Romans 3:23: "For all have sinned and fall short of the glory of God." But I could not believe that every person on earth had sinned. Not that I was perfect, by any means, but I couldn't imagine that there wasn't someone, somewhere, who was without sin.

So there I was, a twenty-three-year-old working for a Christian Chairman of the Board who openly talked about her faith. How could I do the job to the best of my ability without understanding what Christianity was all about? To excel in the position, I decided I would have to learn more about Christianity, so I started to investigate.

An avid reader, I had just finished the novel *Christy* by Catherine Marshall, and I loved it. As with all new authors I liked, my habit was to read everything they had written. Unaware that this was Catherine Marshall's only novel at that time—she primarily wrote books on faith—I began reading the rest of her books in the order she had written them. Each of them chronicled her own walk with Jesus and delved deeper and deeper into spiritual teachings.[3]

One day, I realized that I thought more and more about Jesus. I decided that I needed to do something about it, so I made an appointment with Reverend Earl Harvey, the Methodist minister at the church near my home. When he inquired of me, "Suppose you were to die tonight and stand before God, and He were to ask you, 'Why should I let you into My heaven?' . . . what would you say?" I thought for a moment, and then responded, "I know that it doesn't depend upon anything I have done."

That was all that I knew, not realizing that the answer was Jesus's atoning death. I just understood that Jesus was somehow part of the solution. As Pastor Harvey enlightened me about the salvation message, he continually asked me, "Do you believe this?" and I did! I did not yet know how to articulate that belief, though, or how to relate it in logical progression. At the end of our discussion, I prayed the Sinner's Prayer with Pastor Harvey and began attending his church, a Bible-believing, evangelical body.

As a "new" believer, I took an "Evangelism Explosion" course at the church and gained my first insight into the basics of what Christians believe and how to express that faith. A couple in the course also took me under their wings and became my spiritual parents. What an exciting time this was for me! I was in my honeymoon stage with Jesus. The Bible had come alive. I couldn't stop talking about Jesus and His great gift.

Naturally, I had to share this life-changing news with Mary Kay, who was so sweet and reaffirmed that this was the most important decision a person could ever make.

My very first Mary Kay Seminar was in 1971, the summer I was hired as a temporary secretary. It was held at the Fairmont Hotel in Dallas and attended by 3,800 people. Because the Mary Kay Cosmetics staff was small, everyone had many duties and worked long hours. Having only been a part of Mary Kay Cosmetics for a short time, I didn't understand the culture. The love the sales force had for Mary Kay surprised me greatly. I wondered what kind of company I had joined, but, over the years, I came to realize that this enthusiasm for the career and the appreciation of Mary Kay came from gratitude. She had opened the door for women to find fulfillment in a career, to make money, and to have the flexibility to plan around their families.

As Mary Kay Cosmetics grew into Mary Kay Inc., my responsibilities and roles grew too. My initial position as her Executive Secretary advanced into managing her office staff (it took ten of us at one time to keep up with her). By 1995, the final year that Mary Kay was active in the company, the firm had become so large that our group not only assisted her in all that she did but also was responsible for two company newsletters, one monthly and one weekly, helped process over 18,500 pieces of correspondence directed to Mary Kay personally, fielded almost 16,000 phone calls to her, maintained the company's historical records, and worked at all company events and meetings.

We worked hard, but we didn't mind doing so because we believed in the company's mission of enriching women's lives and we did not want to disappoint Mary Kay. She always set a fast pace. She inspired us, just like she inspired the women in the sales force. We even developed our own mission statement for the department: "To provide personalized support and services to Mary Kay Ash and to be an extension of Mary Kay's image, heart, philosophies, and attitudes to the sales force, other departments, and the public." She called us "the Department of Sunshine and Rainbows."

On February 26, 1996, life at Mary Kay Inc. changed overnight when Mary Kay suffered a stroke that left her unable to talk. Although she tried diligently to speak again with the help of a therapist, she never recovered her voice. Mary Kay was a talented speaker, and it was hard for everyone to accept that she had lost one of her greatest gifts.

That same year, I was appointed Director of the Mary Kay Museum. Since I had lived the Mary Kay Inc. history for so many years—up close and personal with Mary Kay herself—I knew this was the perfect role for me. When people ask why I never joined the Mary Kay sales force after seeing the checks of the top saleswomen, I tell them that God's plan was for me to help Mary Kay Ash build her dream. I was so much younger than Mary Kay and her other assistant, Erma. That was part of God's plan, too. Entrusted with her legacy, I was a walking reservoir of the history of the company and its resources.

The Mary Kay Museum debuted in 1993, having been a dream of Mary Kay's for many years. She had saved everything she thought might someday go into a collection. She would often bring me items and say, "This is for the museum." At the office, we had a closet full of objects from Mary Kay Inc. history and from around the Mary Kay world.

The idea to create a museum came to fruition on one of the many trips Mary Kay and her staff members took to Las Vegas to get ideas for the opening number of the Seminar awards ceremony. Mary Kay loved piano music, and Liberace was the most famous pianist in the United States in the 1980s. Originally celebrated as a concert pianist, his flamboyance and outrageous costumes eventually led to him having his own television show, and he made frequent appearances in Las Vegas.[4] He was a unique showman, and Mary Kay was a huge fan.

One year, Liberace was scheduled to perform when Mary Kay was in Las Vegas, and she wanted to see him. Dale Alexander, Vice President of Sales Development, heard that Liberace had a museum in Las Vegas and asked Mary Kay if she would like to visit. When they arrived, Liberace's brother George—who oversaw the museum—recognized Mary Kay and gave her a personal tour. The collection included everything from Liberace's rhinestone costumes to his customized cars, ornate pianos, and gifts from fans around the world. Dale recounted that there were "toothpicks with the name Liberace carved in them, and mittens knitted with keyboards on the hands." These displayed mementos reminded Mary Kay of the many gifts she had received that had been made with love and sent to her.

Unbeknownst to Mary Kay, the staff had also arranged for her to meet Liberace after his show that evening. Liberace's manager invited her backstage, where Liberace greeted her at his dressing room door in a long, white, flowing robe with a big, fluffy collar. He admired Mary Kay's rings, and she explained to him her trick of coloring her diamonds with a magic marker. They laughed and talked for forty-five minutes.

After Mary Kay returned to Dallas and talked so much about Liberace's museum, company executives decided to build one for Mary Kay Inc.'s thirtieth anniversary as a gift to her. She was highly involved in its design and in selecting the items to be featured, and she was instrumental in sharing the historical events that would be depicted.

Mary Kay had the following message etched in glass at the museum:

Dedicated to the thousands of women
who dared to step out of their comfort zones
and use their God-given talents and abilities,
realizing that God did not have time to make a nobody,
just a somebody.

In 1995, when Mary Kay Inc. moved to a larger headquarters, the museum moved and grew as well. But no provision had been made for maintaining the museum; at the time of Mary Kay's stroke, the museum stagnated. Exhibits were not updated nor artifacts conserved.

When the company appointed me as Museum Director, my first thought was that I knew nothing about running a museum. My second thought was that I could learn. I believed God directed my steps and that He would help me master the subject. I immediately started researching museum studies and discovered some archival courses at the University of Texas at Arlington, where I had earned my bachelor's.

I enrolled in several classes and began attending the annual meeting and statewide workshops of the Texas Association of Museums. After gaining knowledge from both the classes and on-the-job experience, I could say with confidence that I became a professional Museum Director—to the point where I gave lectures at conferences on corporate museums and archives.

During my role as Museum Director, I also assembled documents on Mary Kay traditions and culture, created a book of her quotes by topic for use by our corporate staff, and collected stories about Mary Kay and shared them with others. I often thought about how to pass on my wealth of knowledge that had accumulated over the years; I even fantasized that, like Spock in the *Star Trek* television series, I could do a Vulcan mind meld to leave my knowledge with others. Although our technology wasn't as advanced as that of the Vulcans', with Becky Brown's help, we archived not only the documents that I created as Museum Director, but also Mary Kay's and her son Richard's speeches, timelines for corporate historical events, and articles about Mary Kay Ash, all of which are now preserved for history.

After Mary Kay's stroke, I was concerned and saddened for her, but I saw God show her again and again that He had not left her. I especially recall when a box containing two handcrafted musical angel dolls arrived in our office one day. There was a note inside from the woman who made them, saying that, several years ago, she made these dolls and felt compelled to keep them until God told her to give them to someone special. She had named one of the dolls "Mary," even though the woman did not know Mary Kay and had not had any contact with the company or sales force members. After all these years, she felt that she needed to send them to Mary Kay. Even more amazing, the "Mary" doll played Mary Kay's favorite hymn, "How Great Thou Art." Becky Brown and I took these dolls to Mary Kay, and she was deeply touched because it reaffirmed that God was still with her.

People still ask me if I miss Mary Kay today, and I assure them that she will always be a part of my life because of her influence and example. When the company has hit any milestone since her passing, I have especially wished Mary Kay could have been there to learn about or experience it.

One instance that stands out in my mind was the annual Mary Kay Inc. Circle of Honor Luncheon in 2005, held at the Morton H. Meyerson Symphony Center in Dallas for employees with ten or more years of service to the company. In 2018, over 55 percent of Mary Kay employees had reached this level of tenure.

For many years, the company had a choir that performed at events and on holidays, and Mary Kay was one of its biggest supporters. After her stroke in 1996, the choir went to Mary Kay's house and ministered to her through song, a visit that meant as much to the choir members as it did to Mary Kay. At the 2005 luncheon, three of the choir members were recognized for twenty years of service, and when it came time to pray before the meal, they performed "How Great Thou Art," their voices reverberating throughout the music hall. Looking around the room to observe how others were being affected, I saw so many tenured employees wiping away tears—including myself! As the choir sang, I thought, "How many companies today continue the practice of praying before meals and would allow such a glorifying song to be performed at an event?"

In 2000, I became responsible for managing The Mary Kay Foundation. My passion for its two main goals of eradicating cancer and eliminating domestic violence fueled my desire to grow the foundation so it could help more women.

When I first began managing the foundation, the primary means of raising money was through donations at company events. One of my most significant accomplishments was initiating the MK5K race, which grew from just over three hundred participants in its first year to over thirteen hundred runners and walkers in 2016. For this achievement, I was awarded the Mary Kay Star of Excellence Award. Of course, this achievement would not have been reached if The Mary Kay Foundation team were not such a hard-working, dedicated group as devoted to these causes as I was. Another accomplishment of mine was establishing an ambassador program of sales force members across the United States to help promote and educate others about the Foundation's programs and its goals. Working with the ambassadors was one of the most rewarding roles of my Mary Kay career.

Around the end of 2016, I felt the Lord leading me to step away from my position at Mary Kay Inc. and become more involved in doing His work. I argued with Him that my job was helping people.

However, an inner voice replied, "Yes, but you are not saving souls." From my first years as a Christian, I had wanted to get involved in mission work and devote more time to study and prayer. I realized that was where God was leading me.

Looking back today, I am conscious of what a tremendous blessing working with Mary Kay Ash and her company has been to me, both personally and professionally. I had the best positive role model and mentor to impact my life. Mary Kay influenced the way I raised my children. I grew spiritually and personally. I developed a positive attitude and learned to set goals. I was part of a company that literally changes lives for the better.

During the forty-five years I worked for Mary Kay Inc., I took many company-sponsored personality and management style tests, such as the DISC and Myers-Briggs. People familiar with these tests often ask me what I think Mary Kay's personality type might have been. My response is that Mary Kay had honed so many people skills that she truly became a blend of personality types. She had dominant features because she had to fight for any success she received in a man's world, but she was also sensitive and caring and could be a servant leader. Mary Kay was a visionary and a big-picture thinker. And even though her son Richard balanced her checkbook, she was a most organized person.

The last test I took before leaving Mary Kay Inc. was Gallup's StrengthsFinder—my favorite! Using this test, my biggest strength came out as *belief*. I was accurately pegged. I have a strong belief in God, whose hand was on my roles at Mary Kay Inc., and I also believe it's my responsibility to talk about Mary Kay's Christian legacy. Since these beliefs are a part of my core, retirement didn't mean walking away from the duties God gave me. He prompted me to write this book to show others that an ordinary woman spent her lifetime growing and learning as a servant of God and made a profound impact on millions of lives around the world in the process.

13

A YEAR OF SORROW

His master said to him, "Well done, good and faithful servant.
You have been faithful over a little; I will set you over much.
Enter into the joy of your master."

MATTHEW 25:21

Whatever the reason, someday I will no longer be here.
When that day comes, I know our National Sales Directors
will carry on magnificently in my place.

MARY KAY ASH[1]

Many people will long remember 2001 as a year when the world changed. On September 11, terrorists crashed planes into the Twin Towers of the World Trade Center in New York City and at the Pentagon in Washington, D.C., while brave passengers onboard United Airlines Flight 93 thwarted the terrorists' plans to crash a plane into a fourth location. Their heroic efforts cost them their lives but saved countless others.

2001 became a year of national sorrow, and it was also a year of tremendous personal sorrow for me with the deaths of the two most influential people in my life, my mother and Mary Kay Ash. My mother's health had progressively deteriorated; she suffered from both diabetes and dementia. She then suffered a stroke, and, as a result of her diabetes, developed a wound on her foot that would not heal. She was transferred from nursing home to hospital to nursing home—round and round—until she was finally sent to a wound care center.

The last time I saw my mother, she was hooked up to a host of machines. I looked at her and remembered her wishes. "Lord," I prayed, "you know she always said she didn't want to live like this." That night, I dreamed my mother was young again, frolicking in a field of yellow flowers and shouting with joy, "I am free! I am free!" I was suddenly awakened by the phone ringing; the nurse informed me my mother was going and that I should come to the hospital. Rushing around in a state of shock, I was putting on my shoes when the phone rang again with the news that she was gone. My mother had passed away on my father's birthday, September 1. The grief I felt at losing my beloved mother brought a profound sense of sorrow.

Even in my loss, however, God blessed me. My daughter and Mother's namesake, Mary Elizabeth, was at home at the time, having just graduated from college. She had her first teaching job and would move out at the end of September. Her love for her grandmother and me was a source of strength during those emotional days of preparing for the funeral and sharing what a wonderful woman Mother was. Mother showed her children how to love and how to give. She would recite poetry and silly poems to her children as we grew up, and then did the same to her grandchildren. I still can't pass a purple car without hearing her recite this poem by Gelett Burgess:[2]

I never saw a Purple Cow,
I never hope to see one,
But I can tell you, anyhow,
I'd rather see than be one![3]

She also woke us up in the morning with this poem:

Let us, then, be up and doing,
With a heart for any fate;
Still achieving, still pursuing
Learn to labor and to wait."[4]

I was too emotional to speak at my mother's funeral, so I asked my daughter to speak on my behalf. Her remembrances blessed our family. One of my nieces, Georganna Cabla, also gave a heartfelt message. I still dream of my mom and Mary Kay . . . and my Dad, who passed away in 2005. These dreams are so real that I wake believing they are all still alive, and I can give them a call. However, I know they are alive in the Lord and that I will see them in Heaven.

Although this world is filled with trials, and some years bring more sorrows than others, the hope of the Christian is that we will be reunited with our saved loved ones in death, in a place with no tears or conflict, where all the guilt and remorse for the hurts and misunderstandings that occur between children and parents will be healed and consumed in His enveloping love. Our love will be pure in Heaven.

While I was still mourning my mother, Mary Kay Ash passed away on her favorite holiday, Thanksgiving Day, November 22, 2001. She elected to be cremated, and her urn rests beside the body of her husband Mel. Her memorial service was held on November 28, 2001.

After Mary Kay suffered her stroke, she was unable to attend church. Charlotte McKinney, one of the Mary Kay staff members, had the great idea of taking church to Mary Kay. She arranged for St. Andrew United Methodist Church in Plano, Texas, to minister to Mary Kay in her home and provide communion. Charlotte and her sisters, who together formed a singing group, would visit and sing hymns for Mary Kay.

Other members of the church also visited Mary Kay, sharing brief devotionals with her. The chancel choir, youth choir, and pastors all ministered to Mary Kay. Even though she could not communicate verbally after her stroke, those who saw her expressed to us that she spoke with her eyes and her hands. She took people's hands between her own and focused her attention on them as if the person to whom she was speaking was the only one in the room. When the youth choir visited, she gave each teenager individual attention, and when they left Mary Kay's home, they had tears in their eyes, wanting to come back to see her again.

Due to scheduling conflicts with Mary Kay's home church, Prestonwood Baptist Church, her memorial service was held at Park Cities Baptist Church in Dallas. When I drove onto its campus, I couldn't help but think that it was the perfect place for Mary Kay's memorial—the exterior of the Georgian colonial-style church was pink! The colors in the sanctuary were gold, white, blue, and rose, all colors Mary Kay used in her décor.

At the service, Senior Pastor of Park Cities Baptist Jim Denison delivered these words about Mary Kay's devotion to Christ: "Her personal faith was not an item of religious convenience or Sunday Christianity. From the time she first invited Christ into her life, hers was a deeply personal and passionate devotion to Jesus Christ as Lord . . . It was her faith which gives us hope today. We know that she is with her Heavenly Father, not because her life was singular in its significance, although it was, not because her legacy will continue on for generations to come, although it will, but because she knew Jesus Christ personally."

Reverend Robert Hasley, Senior Pastor at St. Andrew United Methodist Church, remembers when St. Andrew's Reverend Charles

Stokes visited Mary Kay and read Psalm 27 with her. When Stokes finished the reading, he put the Bible on the bed beside her to say a prayer. When he looked up, Mary Kay pushed the Bible toward him because she wanted to hear more. Having been raised in the Baptist church, the Scriptures meant everything to Mary Kay. She always said that her favorite verse was Psalm 56:3: "When I am afraid, I put my trust in you." I am sure she often leaned on this verse following her stroke.

Two of Mary Kay's National Sales Director friends and pioneers of the company represented the sales force in memorializing Mary Kay. Elite Executive National Sales Director Emeritus Dalene White, one of the original nine sales force members when Mary Kay opened the company in 1963, spoke of her forty years of friendship with Mary Kay.[5] They became friends because they both loved cooking and books and they shared recipes and reading recommendations. Her favorite memory was Christmastime in 1963, when Mary Kay held the company Christmas party at her house. The company had only been in business for four months, and the sales force and staff were small. She and Dalene had planned to cook dinner together. When Dalene arrived at Mary Kay's home, Mary Kay greeted her at the door with a smudge of flour on her nose, dressed in her favorite seersucker wrap-around and her favorite frazzled slippers, with her wig hanging on the kitchen doorknob. Dalene left Mary Kay's at 5:30 p.m. to get dressed for dinner and returned at 7:00 p.m. When she came back, Mary Kay looked like a queen, and the house—kitchen and all—was in perfect order, with piles of gifts laying around for everyone.

Dalene also spoke of Mary Kay's humility and faith. When Mel underwent cancer treatments, Dalene would drive the couple to the doctor's office in Mary Kay's car. Mary Kay had her tape deck set to "Why Me, Lord," and would play it every time Dalene chauffeured the two.

Senior National Sales Director Rena Tarbet and Mary Kay had a highly emotional connection because Mary Kay walked with Rena through every step of her lengthy cancer battle. She admired Rena for the courage and positive attitude she maintained throughout the ordeal.[6] As Rena shared, "I've laughed hysterically with her as we ate hot dogs on the street corner in New York and also while eating fried smelt in sunny Spain. I've cried with her over the death of a sister Sales Director with cancer and over the loss of her fur person, Gigi. I've held her hand when she lost her precious daughter, Marylyn, and she held mine when I lost my breast."

It was only fitting that the Mary Kay Choir sang the hymns Mary Kay had chosen for her service, as well as a song titled "On Silver Wings," inspired by her favorite poem, "Premonition." At the end of this song, Mary Kay's voice reverberated throughout the sanctuary as they played a recording of her reciting this poem, prompting many memories among the attendees.

As Dalene prepared to close her remarks, she reminded everyone of Mary Kay's impact on so many lives: "She never really understood that everywhere she went, she left a part of herself in the heart of everyone she met. And if we could hear her voice right now, she would be saying, 'Pass it on.'"

14

LEGACY

I will sing of the steadfast love of the Lord, forever;
with my mouth I will make known your
faithfulness to all generations.

PSALM 89:1

Years ago, I worried about what might happen to the
company if I was no longer here. I felt a deep responsibility
to the thousands and thousands of people involved with Mary
Kay Cosmetics. The company had come so far so quickly that I
wanted to be sure it could grow and prosper without me.

MARY KAY ASH[1]

After Mary Kay's stroke, I reflected on all that had been achieved from
1971—when I first started working at Mary Kay Cosmetics—to 1996,
when she could no longer play an active role in the company she
loved. It seemed impossible that Mary Kay could have accomplished
so much. I am not talking about the billion-dollar company that
bears her name, but about all the lives she touched. She met an in-
credible number of people, participated in countless trips, personally
answered mountains of correspondence, wrote handwritten thank
you notes, sympathy cards, and congratulatory notes to hundreds of
people a year, and wrote weekly and monthly articles for Mary Kay

Inc. publications. She even wrote her own speeches to ensure that her heart would be in the words she spoke.

As her Executive Assistant and the manager of her staff, I worked by Mary Kay's side through the growth of the company. God impressed upon me that He had anointed both of us—her for the work of Christian leadership to women, and me for supporting her in that role. Working long hours, I had tremendous responsibility and balanced multiple projects, all while raising three children. Only through the grace of God could I have managed all that.

Mary Kay never sought accolades, though, and was never impressed by them. She always felt that her greatest achievement was the thousands of lives that had been, and continue to be, enriched by the Mary Kay opportunity. Changing people's lives through her company was her motivation and the achievement closest to her heart. She was grateful that God used Mary Kay Inc. to fulfill the dream she had in 1963 of providing women with opportunity and flexibility in a career.

Throughout the years, Mary Kay experienced successes, challenges, and setbacks in her career and personal life. As she would say, "It is not so much what happens to us as how we react to what happens that makes a difference." Mary Kay taught people to have a positive attitude and to look for the silver lining in every tough situation. She would reminisce on the challenges in her life and remark on how God used those challenges to prepare her to found Mary Kay Inc. This reminds me of Paul's famous verse in Romans 8:28: "And we know that for those who love God all things work together for good, for those who are called according to his purpose."

The truth of that Scripture could be seen even in the silver lining of the stroke she suffered: she was able to see the company she founded grow strong and flourish even when she was no longer its driving presence. After her stroke, Richard brought videos of the

Seminars from Mary Kay subsidiaries to her home so she could watch the successes of women from all cultures in comfort. I can imagine her joy. This was the "good" God brought to her life once she could no longer work. After she passed away in 2001, company wholesale sales increased from $1 billion to $1.4 billion, and the sales force grew from 437,000 to 900,000 women worldwide.

Ray Patrick, President of Mary Kay Canada, shared with me that when he once told Mary Kay she must be very happy her dream had come true, she responded, "I won't be happy until the third and fourth generations of women are taking advantage of this opportunity." The good news is that she *can* be happy because the daughters and granddaughters of sales force members she once knew now pursue their own Mary Kay careers. If Mary Kay were here today, I know she would be dreaming about the next generations of Mary Kay sales force members around the world.

In thinking about all the lives Mary Kay has touched since the company was founded in 1963, I am reminded of a very special birthday gift Mary Kay received after her stroke. In early 2000, the Mary Kay video department produced a beautiful film to promote the launch of the TimeWise skin care line. In one scene, a woman opens a floral box, and instead of roses, butterflies emerge and flutter around her. One of the Beauty Consultants attending a career conference that year wanted to recreate this experience for Mary Kay, and she found a company that would send butterflies through the mail.

Coordinating this gift was not an easy task because the butterflies had to be opened within a certain timeframe. Nancy Thomason and I worked together to make this unusual gift a surprise for Mary Kay. Nancy took Mary Kay to a dental appointment, leaving a note for the UPS driver to leave the package at the door. When Nancy and Mary Kay returned to her home, they found a note stating that the box could not be delivered without a signature.

Nancy immediately called UPS, and the dispatcher was amazed. "That package is for *the* Mary Kay Ash?" Nancy confirmed that yes, it was, and the driver was back in thirty minutes with a flat box marked on all sides with the phrase, "Do Not Crush."

Mary Kay's birthday guests arrived, and Nancy left the package for Bob Knight, a member of the security team, to handle. Intrigued by the mysterious box and concerned for Mary Kay's safety, he cautiously opened the package to find dozens of small white packets. When he unfolded one, a butterfly started to move, and then emerged onto his hand. He then had a nurse bring Mary Kay out onto the terrace.

As Bob recalls, "Each butterfly lingered on [Mary Kay's] face and clothes for a few minutes before flying off, and then I would open a few more packets," Bob remembers. "Nearly all of the butterflies stayed right there in her yard, which led to a lake behind her house. It was a moving sight to see so many butterflies filling our view, reflecting in the water. We could tell Mary Kay felt peaceful and at ease with them resting on her. She had a big smile on her face the whole time."

Those of us who have been influenced by Mary Kay are like those butterflies. We landed in her world, were blessed by her warmth, and now have flown on to new opportunities. However, a part of her will always remain in our lives. More than a half-century after Mary Kay founded her business, the principles and philosophies she espoused are carried on in the hearts of thousands of Mary Kay employees, retirees, and current Mary Kay Independent Beauty Consultants. She didn't just plant a career in their hearts; she planted hope, opportunities for growth, and a better way of life for their families. Mary Kay can also be happy that the company she founded continues spreading its philosophy around the world, and that The Mary Kay Foundation is solid and secure.

Even though Mary Kay Ash is no longer on earth to see the results, her legacy lives on through the many women who never even heard her speak, who never met her, or even caught a glimpse of her, but have incorporated her teachings into their lives. Mary Kay Inc. now has young, new leaders who have wholeheartedly adopted her philosophies.

Among these new leaders is Senior National Sales Director Kristin Myers, who joined Mary Kay Inc. in January 2002, a year after Mary Kay's death.[2] When Kristin first heard about the company, she wondered, "Can this be real?" Curious, she went to the library and checked out every book Mary Kay had written, as well as any books that featured her. As Kristin told me, "I found Mary Kay to be a fascinating woman who had endured hardships. She was humble, responsible, and had a good work ethic." As she continued learning more about Mary Kay's life and her company, she discovered that the philosophies of the company matched her own personal values. "I believed that if I really could keep God first, I would have found the golden nugget. Mary Kay created a family environment that filled my heart as a mother. I felt completed. I could be a mother and have a career that coincided with my values."

As a child, Kristin's grandmother had been her spiritual mentor. However, she discovered in Mary Kay a woman who could show her how to be a Christian businesswoman. "My spiritual growth was nourished in Mary Kay. I was constantly surrounded by lessons on how to live my principles. I found great mentors and positive encouragement."

Even though she never met Mary Kay, Kristin is committed to keeping Mary Kay's legacy alive. "I play Mary Kay videos at every event, and people always cry," she says. "When she speaks, her words and motives are so pure. She is speaking not to gain, but to give. She speaks directly to our hearts. In our national area, we want to practice her principles, realizing she gleaned these principles from the Bible. Like Jesus, she taught in stories and parables. Her words create spiritual curiosity and lead to changed lives."

Senior National Sales Director Dayana Polanco, who is of Cuban descent and lives in Miami, is another new young leader in the company.[3] She has taken the Mary Kay opportunity beyond the borders of the United States, with sales force members in seven countries. Before joining Mary Kay, Dayana was working for the State Department as a Resettlement Specialist, helping refugees who had come to the United States for political reasons adjust to their new lives here. After hosting a skin care class for one of her coworkers, Dayana fell in love with the Mary Kay products, philosophies, and company. Dayana had never been introduced to a company that shared her values. She was also impressed when she learned that, through a Mary Kay career, one could grow as a leader and help people. "All she was saying connected with my heart," Dayana recalls.

Four months later, Dayana became a Sales Director and resigned from her position at the State Department. Mary Kay's principles became a reference for Dayana to lead her life without compromising her values, and Mary Kay became her example of what a Christian businesswoman should be. Before Mary Kay, Dayana had no example for how successful women should act. Now, she is very aware that she has an opportunity for people to know Jesus Christ through her example. "I don't preach; rather, I build relationships," she notes. "Through living as a Christian, I show people how they can have better lives for themselves."

National Sales Director Patrice Moore Smith also represents the new generation at Mary Kay Inc.[4] When she began her Mary Kay career, Patrice was an educator and was married with three children, including a set of twins. Thinking about their college educations, she decided to change careers because of the limited earning potential in education. However, when she entered the business world, Patrice discovered that the priorities in corporate America are job first, job second, and job third.

Unhappy with this tradeoff of job over faith and family, Patrice began thinking of her dream job, one where she could make money but not have to sacrifice her personal life. She began praying that God would guide her footsteps toward such a career. Patrice's husband is a pastor, and at a pastor's conference they attended, she met a woman who offered her a Mary Kay business card. The woman then shared amazing things about Mary Kay Inc. "Before meeting with her, I only knew that Mary Kay was an excellent product line. When I heard about the company, I thought, '*Is this real?*'"

Patrice fell in love with the philosophy, principles, and ability to help other women. She was excited to show others that they didn't have to sacrifice their families for a career: they did not have to choose between either/or, but could instead have both/and. A pastor's daughter, Patrice was raised in the church, but Mary Kay Inc. has drawn her into a closer walk of faith. "Being an entrepreneur is a faith walk," she says. "I have seen God provide, and I have seen Him change lives. My journey has been enlarged and blessed by the fact that I have been surrounded by women of extreme faith. I want to preserve for posterity and perpetuity the company's philosophies. That is what sets us apart and makes us different."

Senior National Sales Director Julia Burnett, who joined Mary Kay Inc. in 2002, built her Mary Kay business in Lexington, Kentucky.[5] She was first drawn to the company because of its strong female leaders, and, at the age of twenty-four, she realized that she had been introduced to an exceptional opportunity. Julia felt overwhelmed with gratitude at Mary Kay's vision and courage. She had found a company where women could reach success and keep their priorities in order.

A nominal Christian before she joined Mary Kay Inc., Julia was surrounded by Christian businesswomen who lived positive lives, and through their example, she discovered a personal relationship with

Jesus. When others ask about the secret to her success in the company, she doesn't hesitate to proclaim, "I truly believe with all my heart that my area was divinely chosen by God. I pray daily that God will send me women who love Him or want to love Him."

The husband of one of Julia's Beauty Consultants, a youth pastor who has studied the early Christian church in detail, has reinforced her belief that being God-centered has created a special connection among her group. "This community of believers is more like the early church than any church I have attended," he once told her, impressed with the way her group cared and prayed for each other.

Julia also knows the important role traditions play in bonding new Beauty Consultants to the company. She focuses on the Go-Give Spirit in her area and hosts a culture night at Seminar, bringing in speakers who personally knew Mary Kay Ash. "I have a young area, and millennials love the legacy, but they don't know much about the history of Mary Kay. I have panels where my more tenured Sales Directors share what it means to build a Mary Kay business on the Golden Rule."

All four of these young women helping to lead Mary Kay Inc. today embody two qualities I saw in Mary Kay—faith and humility. Despite her phenomenal success, Mary Kay remained down-to-earth. Mary Kay was as genuine in 1996 as she was when I first met her in 1971, and based on my firsthand experiences with her over those many years, I can say with assurance that there were two reasons for her humility. First, she knew that God had His hand on Mary Kay Inc., and that He had chosen her and prepared her for the mission of helping women. Mary Kay always gave credit to Him because she realized that all blessings come from Him.

Second, Mary Kay understood that she could not have built such a successful company in such a short time by herself, but that it took a team to create something great. Whenever someone would ask Mary

Kay about "her" company, she would always correct that person and say that this was not just her company. She gave credit to the dedicated sales force and employees who helped achieve her dream for the success of the organization.

Because she was so genuine, Mary Kay made a great role model. When she saw others limit their availability, she would tell me, "I never want to live in an Ivory Tower." She didn't believe in what she called "executivitus." She realized that when people are well-known, they tend to think more highly of themselves than they should. "Never believe your own publicity" was another motto by which she lived.

When I think about Mary Kay's continued influence in my life and the lives of others, I am reminded of an illustration from Joyce Landorf Heatherly, a Christian author popular in the 1980s. She wrote *Balcony People*, a book about encouragement.[6] Joyce believes that we encounter two types of people in our lives: evaluators and affirmers. Evaluators break our spirits by their critical or judgmental evaluations. Joyce calls such individuals "basement people" because they pull us down with comments like, "You are not going to make it." They tell us we can't do this or that and drop subtle—or sometimes not so subtle—hints about our inferior qualities, attempting to damage our self-esteem.

In contrast, affirmers are "balcony people." They discern what's best in others, looking for noble, honorable, and good qualities. They see the talents and abilities in those around them, then proceed to tell those people how they admire these traits. They make others see themselves as worthwhile, nurtured, and loved.

Joyce believed that a balcony filled with people who are practically hanging over the rail and cheering us on runs all around us in our conscious minds. I was particularly inspired by the way Joyce ended her book, asking that we picture the people in our balconies. After reading this book, I hope that, when you close your eyes and look for the people in your balcony, Mary Kay Ash will be one of them. If so, she would tell you:

> *I have a premonition that soars on silver wings.*
> *It's a dream of your accomplishment of many wondrous things.*
> *I do not know beneath which sky or where you'll challenge fate.*
> *I only know it will be high.*
> *I only know it will be great!* [7]

In the last chapter of her autobiography, "Leaving a Legacy," Mary Kay advised, "People change and even products change. But over the course of time it's the strength of a company's philosophy that will determine whether or not it endures . . . Years ago, I worried about what might happen to the company if I were no longer involved . . . The company had come so far so quickly that I wanted to be certain it would grow and prosper without me . . . I was possessed with the desire to leave a legacy. I know now that my legacy is assured. The company has my name, but it also has a life of its own. And its life's blood is the philosophy that many thousands of women have made a part of their lives."[8]

So much has changed since the company opened its doors in 1963. The products have evolved; the marketing plan has been updated; new technology has opened the door to new ways of doing business. Mary Kay and those who founded the company with her are no longer at the helm. In 1963, women came to Mary Kay Cosmetics because they wanted to get out of the house and have a fulfilling career. Today, women come to Mary Kay Inc. because they want to get back *into* the house and have a fulfilling career. But what has not changed is the dedication of those who believe in Mary Kay's philosophies and wish to carry on her principles.

Mary Kay Ash lived her life driven by her principles—her trust in God, her belief in the Golden Rule, and her faith in women. She blazed a trail and left a legacy. Generations of lives have been changed, and I count myself blessed that my family and I are among those impacted by her witness. If you, too, have been touched by her words and example, remember that she would ask you to pass it on.

APPENDIX A

Book Suggestions for the New Christian and Those Who Want to Go Deeper

For the New Christian:

New Living Translation of the Bible: For any Christian, the most important book to read is the Bible. There is no substitute for Bible reading. This translation is in modern English, translated from the original texts. Scholars translated entire thoughts rather than word for word, which makes it easy to read and understand. Christians who have never before read the Bible or been exposed to the message of Christianity should start in the New Testament.

Closer Walk New Testament by Paula Kirk, from Walk Thru The Bible Ministries

Mere Christianity by C.S. Lewis

The Confessions of St. Augustine by St. Augustine, translated by John K. Ryan

The Case for Christ: A Journalist's Personal Investigation of the Evidence for Jesus by Lee Strobel

A Man Called Peter: The Story of Peter Marshall and *Beyond Ourselves* by Catherine Marshall

Crazy Love: Overwhelmed by a Relentless God by Frances Chan

Experiencing God: Knowing and Doing the Will of God by Claude V. King, Henry T. Blackaby, and Richard Blackaby

For Those Who Want to Go Deeper:

In Pursuit of God and *The Pursuit of Man: The Divine Conquest of the Human Heart* by A.W. Tozer

On the Incarnation by St. Athanasius of Alexandria

The Christian's Secret of a Happy Life by Hannah Whitall Smith

The Cost of Discipleship by Dietrich Bonhoeffer

Idols of the Heart: Learning to Long for God Alone by Elyse Fitzpatrick

Total Forgiveness by R. T. Kendall

Celebration of Discipline: The Path to Spiritual Growth by Richard J. Foster

Trusting God: Even When Life Hurts by Jerry Bridges

A Testament of Devotion by Thomas Raymond Kelly

APPENDIX B

Jalapeño Dressing (For Turkey)[1]

Serves: 12

This is the recipe Mary Kay is most famous for. It has been published in many celebrity cookbooks through the years. Her family says she made two versions of dressing every Thanksgiving. One had her favorite jalapeños and juice which she called "the good stuff," and one—to accommodate children and delicate stomachs—was jokingly named "worthless"!

INGREDIENTS:

Corn Bread

- 2 cups yellow cornmeal
- 2 cups flour, sifted
- ⅓ cup sugar
- 8 teaspoons baking powder
- 1 teaspoon salt
- 2 eggs
- 2 cups milk
- ½ cup soft shortening

Dressing

- ¼–½ cup cooking oil or bacon drippings (if available)
- 1 bunch green onions, chopped
- ½ whole stalk celery, including leaves, chopped
- 1 cup water
- 3 cups cornbread, from recipe above, crumbled
- 4 cups day-old bread, crumbled
- 2–3 cups turkey broth or more as needed for moist texture
- 1 cup jalapeño juice
- salt and pepper to taste
- chopped jalapeños to taste

Directions:

Sift together cornmeal, flour, sugar, baking powder, and salt into bowl. Add eggs, milk, and shortening. Beat until smooth, about 1 minute. Bake in two 8-inch square baking pans in a preheated 425° oven for 20–25 minutes. Sauté onions and celery in cooking oil or bacon drippings. Add 1 cup water, cover, cook until barely tender, about 7 minutes. Combine with last six ingredients. Add water until right consistency, if necessary. Stuff turkey with dressing and place excess dressing in greased casserole and bake at 350° for 30 minutes.

APPENDIX C

Wham-Bam Cookies[1]

Ingredients:

- 1 cup butter
- 1 cup sugar
- 1 egg
- 2 cups flour
- ½ teaspoon baking soda

Directions:

Cream butter and sugar; add egg. Sift flour and baking soda and add to mixture. Place small bits of dough rolled in tiny balls on ungreased cookie sheet. Dip small juice glass in flour and WHAM-BAM! (Hit lightly to flatten). Bake 4 minutes, or until cookie is slightly brown around the edges, at 400°. Allow to cool 1 minute and remove immediately. Yield: 100 cookies.

Oatmeal Crisps[2]

Ingredients:

- 1 cup shortening
- 1 cup brown sugar
- 1 cup granulated sugar
- 2 eggs
- 1 teaspoon vanilla
- 1½ cups flour
- 1 teaspoon salt
- 1 teaspoon baking soda
- 3 cups quick oats
- ½ cup chopped nuts

DIRECTIONS:

Thoroughly cream shortening and sugars. Add eggs and vanilla. Beat well. Sift together flour, salt, and baking soda. Add to creamed mixture. Beat well. Stir in oats and nuts; mix. Form dough in roll 1 to 1½ inches in diameter; wrap in waxed paper. Chill. With sharp knife, slice cookies about ½ inch thick. Bake on ungreased cookie sheet 10 minutes at 350°. Yield: 5 dozen.

APPENDIX D

Lord, I Need To Be A Winner[1]

Lord, I need to be a winner
not for me, but for You—
People are watching and I am
the example they will follow.

Lord, I need to be a winner—
to show someone else the way.
I can touch more lives by being a success
so, I need to succeed today.

Lord, I need to be a winner—
and I'm willing to do my share
but knowing that all things good come from You—
I need to know You're there.

Lord, I need to be a winner—
every day You give me life—
and with Your leadership and Your strength
I know I can succeed in my business,
and in my personal life.

And Lord, when You help me win—
and I stand to tell my story—
I'll always remember to give unto You
the Praise,
the Honor and
the Glory!

J. S. "Kirk" Kirkpatrick

APPENDIX E

I watched for twenty-five years as Mary Kay Ash submitted to God's call for her life. This call changed the lives of countless women as they discovered what Mary Kay meant by putting God first. Like Kathy Helou, Birgit Johnson, and myself, women discovered the wonderful joy of coming to know Jesus as our personal Savior. Some women in the company have recommitted their lives, while others have embarked upon a path of great spiritual growth.

Mary Kay wanted to enable women to have the financial freedom to send their children to college, travel the world, and give generously to any causes close to their hearts. But she wasn't just concerned about the temporal lives of others; she was concerned with their eternal lives. My hope is that this book has challenged you to consider your own walk with God. Can you hear Mary Kay asking you, as she did Kathy Helou, "Do you know who Jesus is?" Perhaps she is telling you, "You are the only Bible some people will ever read," as she told Birgit Johnson. Perhaps her life inspires you to live out your life with God at the center.

As Mary Kay knew, the secret to a contented life on earth and an eternal home in the Kingdom of Heaven is Jesus. You might be wondering who Jesus is and what becoming a Christian means.

As I mentioned earlier in this book, at the end of my spiritual quest, I visited a Methodist minister who asked me, "If you were to stand before God today and He asked you, 'Why should I let you into my Heaven?'. . . what would you say?" I knew it had nothing to do with me, and it had everything to do with Jesus, but I didn't fully understand God's plan for salvation. When I accepted Christ as my personal Savior, I became what Christians call "born again," which means born into the Kingdom of Heaven. That was the start of my spiritual walk.

If you would like to know more about this Jesus whom Mary Kay shared and served, let me introduce you to Him. He was the perfect man because He came to earth to take the burden of our sins and put them on His shoulders. Sin is something our society does not like to think or talk about, especially when it comes to personal sin. But everyone sins, including Mary Kay, you, and me. As Scripture tells us in Romans 3:23, "All have sinned and fall short of the glory of God." I had never really thought much about sin, and certainly not my sin. I was a good person from a good family. However, when I looked at my life and compared it to the holiness of God, I realized that there was no way that I could make myself good enough to stand in the presence of God. One of the first things I learned is that I needed a savior.

The good news of Jesus Christ is simple. Jesus died on the cross for the sins of mankind. Salvation is a gift from God. All you have to do is accept this gift. If you believe Jesus died on the cross for your sins and pray the simple prayer below, you will experience the forgiveness of God. All you must do is sincerely say to Jesus the following prayer:

> Most Holy God, I know that I have sinned against you. You are holy, and my sin separates me from you. I am grateful that you have provided me a Savior in Jesus Christ who died for me. He took my sins upon Himself so that I could come to you with a clean heart. I believe that He died on the cross for me. I put my life in Your hands. From this day forward, help me to live for you. Amen.

If you sincerely prayed this prayer, welcome to the family of God! Your next steps are to 1) seek out and attend a church that has Biblical teachings, and 2) start reading the Bible. If you don't have one, I suggest the New Living Translation. Begin your reading with the book of Matthew in the New Testament.

If you have made a commitment to Jesus as a result of learning about Mary Kay's witness, please let me know at passitonbycook@ gmail.com.

ENDNOTES

PREFACE

1. Kurt Kaiser, "History of Hymns: 'Pass It On,'" Discipleship Ministries: The United Methodist Church, Published July 2, 2014, https://www.umcdiscipleship.org/resources/history-of-hymns-pass-it-on.
2. I am confident that readers will see the affection and high regard I have for Mary Kay Inc., where I worked for so many years, but I also want to make it clear that my book is my own work and is not endorsed by the company.
3. Lorrie Moore, *Who Will Run the Frog Hospital?* (New York City: Knopf, 1994), 25.

1. MARY KAY'S STORY

1. Mary Kay Ash, *You Can Have It All* (Rocklin, CA: Prima Publishing, 1995), 7.
2. Sue Sheridan, *Teachers Make a Difference.* (Houston, TX: Harris County Department of Education, 1991), 10.
3. Morris L. Mayer, *Direct Selling in the United States: A Commentary and Oral History*, (Washington, D.C., The Direct Selling Education Foundation, 1995), 12.
4. *Direct Selling in the United States*, 13.
5. The Mary Kay sales force consists of independent contractors who are not employees of Mary Kay Inc. When I wrote for Mary Kay Inc., company policy dictated that the word "Independent" must be inserted before the words "Beauty Consultant," "Sales Director," or "National Sales Director." I am noting this here out of respect to the Mary Kay legal department. However, to continually repeat the word "Independent" throughout this memoir could become tedious to the reader.
6. Mary Kay Ash, *Mary Kay* (New York City: HarperCollins Publishers, Inc., 1981), 33.
7. *Mary Kay*, 60.
8. These figures are from one of my speeches that I gave for the company, and I obtained them from company records to which I now don't have access. These figures should be public record since they were involved in Mary Kay going public.
9. Mary Kay Ash, interview by Morley Safer, *60 Minutes Overtime*, CBS, 1979.
10. Dattatraya Muzumdar, "Neurosurgery in the Past and Future. An Appraisal," *Annals of medicine and surgery* 1, (2012): https://www.ncbi.nlm.nih.gov/pmc/articles/PMC4523152.

11. Jim Underwood, *More Than A Pink Cadillac* (New York City: McGraw-Hill, Inc., 2003), xi.
12. For an extended list of Mary Kay's awards and honors, visit www.marykay-legacy.com.
13. "Mission," Horatio Alger Association of Distinguished Americans Inc., accessed April 18, 2020, https://horatioalger.org/about-us.

2. Mary Kay's Personal Life

1. Mary Kay Ash, *You Can Have It All*, (Rocklin, CA: Prima Publishing, 1995), xii.
2. You can find Mary Kay's jalapeño cornbread recipe in Appendix B.
3. Mary Kay's staff hid Mr. Goodbars on the plane and in her hotel suite when they were traveling so that Mary Kay would find them in unexpected places.
4. Mary Kay Ash, *You Can Have It All*, (Rocklin, CA: Prima Publishing, 1995), 244.
5. Doretha Dingler started her Mary Kay career in 1965. She debuted as a Sales Director in 1967 and as a National Sales Director in 1974. When she retired in January 2003, she was one of only five sales force members to have earned the title of Number One National Sales Director Worldwide.
6. Doretha Dingler, *In Pink: The Personal Story of a Mary Kay Pioneer Who Made History Shaping a New Path to Success for Women*, (Scottsdale, Arizona: Brevin, LLC, 2012), 130-31.
7. Pat Danforth started her Mary Kay career in 1973. Pat says she wanted the position of Sales Director because of "the suit, the scoop, and the loot." She debuted as a Sales Director in 1975 and as a National Sales Director in 1990.
8. Wilda DeKerlegand began her Mary Kay career in May 1974. She became a Sales Director in November 1979 and a National Sales Director in November 2002. When people ask Wilda her denomination, she says that she is Catholic with a lot of Baptist sprinkled into her because of Mary Kay Ash's influence. Mary Kay was also a big fan of Wilda's pecan pies!
9. Kendra Crist Cross joined Mary Kay in January 1977. She became a Sales Director in 1980 and a National Sales Director in 2005. She strives to live by Mary Kay's motto, "Don't talk the talk if you don't walk the walk."
10. Arlene Lenarz joined Mary Kay Inc. in 1972. She became a Sales Director in 1973 and a National Sales Director in 1977. Mary Kay taught Arlene that there would always be obstacles in life, but she should always keep her eye on the goal.
11. Today we would call them Spanx.

3. Mary Kay's Typical Day

1. Mary Kay Ash, *Mary Kay*, 3rd ed. (New York City: HarperCollins Publishers, Inc., 1994), 187.
2. James Clear, "The Ivy Lee Method: The Daily Routine Experts Recommend for Peak Productivity," James Clear, Accessed April 9, 2021, https://jamesclear.com/ivy-lee.
3. Most sources quote this figure as $25,000; however, in Mary Kay's book and in her speeches, she always used the figure of $35,000.

4. Mary Kay the Teacher

1. Mary Kay Ash, *You Can Have It All*, (Rocklin, CA: Prima Publishing, 1995), 9.
2. Emily McLaughlin joined Mary Kay Inc. in 1971. She became a Sales Director in 1972 and a National Sales Director in February 1979. She was the first Sales Director in New Jersey.
3. LaQueta McCollum-Fisher began her Mary Kay career in June 1965. She became a Sales Director in 1968 and a National Sales Director in 2002. Her business allowed her to add money to her family's budget and be at home with her two daughters. Her daughters' friends told her that they always enjoyed coming to her house because she had dinner on the table every night and that their household was so "normal."
4. Mary Kay Ash, *You Can Have It All*, (Rocklin, CA: Prima Publishing, 1995), xii.
5. Mickey Ivey began her Mary Kay career in 1967. She became a Sales Director in November 1969 and a National Sales Director in 1981. Her mother was killed tragically in a car accident that also left her son in a coma for eighteen days. Mary Kay called Mickey every day to let her know she was praying for her.
6. Sue Kirkpatrick began her Mary Kay career in March 1975. She became a Sales Director in 1976 and a National Sales Director in 1992. She led a top unit for fifteen years, nine times as number one, and six times in the number two spot.
7. Phyllis Pottinger joined Mary Kay Inc. in 1984 and became a Sales Director in 1985. She debuted as a National Sales Director on August 1, 2013—her birthday. Phyllis earned the privilege of the pink Cadillac multiple times, but she never took it because she did not like to drive. She built her business by taking taxis and the train into New York City.
8. Maria Alvarez began her Mary Kay business in late 1975. She became a Sales Director in August 1976 and a National Sales Director in 1991. Whenever I saw Maria, she would try to convince me to join her team. I never told Mary Kay!
9. The name of the beauty show has changed over the years from "skin care class" to "Mary Kay party."

10. Cheryl Warfield began her Mary Kay career in May 1973. She became a Sales Director in 1974 and a National Sales Director in 1982. She was thirty-one years old when she became the thirty-first National Sales Director.

11. Anne Newbury began her Mary Kay career in July 1969 and built her business in the Boston area. She became a Sales Director in 1971 and a National Sales Director in 1976. In her 1981 autobiography, Mary Kay says of Anne: "More than any other individual, Anne has been responsible for helping our company grow in Canada."

12. Mary Kay Ash, *Mary Kay*, (New York City: Harper & Row, Publishers, Inc., 1981), 137.

5. MARY KAY THE LEADER

1. Mary Kay Ash, *Mary Kay on People Management*, (New York City: Warner Books, Inc., 1984), xix.

2. Jim Underwood, *More Than a Pink Cadillac*, (New York City: McGraw-Hill, Inc., 2003), 196.

3. Mary Kay Ash, *Mary Kay on People Management*, (New York City: Warner Books Inc., 1984), 91.

4. Anna Ewing joined Mary Kay Inc. in 1965. She became a Sales Director in 1965 and a National Sales Director in 1982. Mary Kay called Anna "The Idea Lady" because the company adopted many of the suggestions she made.

5. Katie McLaughlin, "5 Things Women Couldn't Do in the Workplace in the 1960s," *CNN* online, last modified August 25, 2014, https://www.cnn.com/2014/08/07/living/sixties-women-5-things/index.html.

6. "Women's Earnings as a Percentage of Men's, 1951-2013," *InfoPlease*, last modified February 28, 2017, https://www.infoplease.com/womens-earnings-percentage-mens-1951-2013.

7. "5 Things Women Couldn't Do in the Workplace in the 1960s."

8. Kathy Helou began her Mary Kay business in November 1981. She became a Sales Director within eleven months, earning her first pink Cadillac. In 1993, she became a National Sales Director. Kathy says of Mary Kay, "Like Billy Graham, her message never changed. She was never diverted from her message of becoming our best and helping people."

9. In *More Than A Pink Cadillac*, on page xiii, Dick Bartlett expressed his thoughts on this when he wrote, "But there was something more [than listening] her leadership style required of me: to *think like a woman*. Mary Kay reminded me on more than one occasion that I was 'thinking like a man' on some issue. That mindset simply won't cut it in a company with an independent sales force of nearly a million women, and so I and other males learned what, for lack of a better term, might be called empathetic thinking."

10. In 2008 *Mary Kay on People Management* was revised and renamed *The Mary Kay Way: Timeless Principles from America's Greatest Woman Entrepreneur*. In 2019 it was issued again as *Mary Kay on People Management*.

11. Sandy Miller joined Mary Kay Inc. in November 1974. She debuted as a Sales Director in 1976 and as a National Sales Director in 1996. This letter was included in her emeritus speech at a Leadership Conference. Knowing that there were eight hundred new Sales Directors who had never been under Mary Kay's tutelage, Sandy prayed that God would give her a message that showed them Mary Kay's character.

12. Jim Underwood, *More Than A Pink Cadillac*, (New York City: McGraw-Hill, Inc., 2003), 137.

6. Mary Kay the Rock Star

1. Mary Kay Ash, "Mary Kay Ash 700 Club Interviews," interview by Pat Robertson and Ben Kinchlow, *The 700 Club*, Christian Broadcasting Network (CBN), November 6, 1981.

2. "Mary Kay Ash 700 Club Interviews."

3. Patricia Bauer, "Robert Harold Schuller," *Britannica Academic*, s.v., (2015): accessed March 23, 2021, https://academic-eb-com.eres.qnl.qa/levels/collegiate /article/Robert-Harold-Schuller/624610.

7. Mary Kay the Philanthropist

1. Mary Kay Ash, *You Can Have It All*, (Rocklin, CA: Prima Publishing, 1995), 216-17.

2. R. L. Sharpe, "A Bag of Tools," Poetry Nook, accessed March 23, 2021, https:// www.poetrynook.com/poem/bag-tools.

3. Mary Kay Ash, *You Can Have It All*, (Rocklin, CA: Prima Publishing, 1995), 209.

8. Mary Kay the Steward

1. Mary Kay Ash, *Mary Kay on People Management*, (New York City: Warner Books, Inc., 1984), 151.

2. History.com Editors, "Great Recession," History, A&E Television Network, October 11, 2019, https://www.history.com/topics/21st-century/recession.

3. Sharon Tahaney, *Living a Rich Life: Achieving personal, financial and spiritual abundance following Mary Kay's laws of living rich*, (New York City: Forbes Custom Publishing Inc., 2000).

4. Pat cautions those who want to try this trick as it will ruin costume jewelry.

9. The Mary Kay Culture

1. Mary Kay Ash, *Mary Kay on People Management*, (New York City: Warner Books, Inc., 1984), 4.
2. Information on the Direct Selling Association can be found at www.dsa.org.
3. Ann Sullivan joined Mary Kay Inc. in August 1965 and debuted as a Sales Director in 1968. She was Missouri State Queen for eleven out of thirteen years and became a National Sales Director in January 1989. Mary Kay became so well-known that shopping was difficult for her; since she and Ann had similar tastes, Ann would bring Mary Kay outfits and jewelry to supplement her wardrobe. Ann passed away in December 2020 at the age of 102.
4. Mary Kay Ash, *You Can Have It All,* (Rocklin, CA: Prima Publishing, 1995), 162.
5. Mary Kay Ash, *Mary Kay*, 3rd ed., (New York City: HarperCollins Publishers, Inc., 1994), 151-152.
6. Stuart E. Jacobsen, *Only the Best: A Celebration of Gift Giving in America*, (New York City: Harry N. Abrams, Inc., 1985), 47.
7. See Appendix C for a couple of these recipes, which were featured in the company cookbook: Mary Kay Cosmetics, *Cooking with Mary Kay*, (Austin, TX: Hart Graphics, 1985).
8. Claude Steiner, *The Original Warm Fuzzy Tale*, (Fawnskin, CA: Jalmar Press, 1970).
9. Mary Kay Ash, *Mary Kay,* 3rd ed., (New York City: HarperCollins Publishers, Inc., 1994), 192.

10. Mary Kay Goes Global

1. Mary Kay Ash, *Pearls of Wisdom: A Personal Perspective with Mary Kay Ash—What You Send Into the Lives of Others*, read by Mary Kay Ash (Dallas: Mary Kay Cosmetics, Inc., 1992), cassette.
2. Gladys Reyes began her Mary Kay business in March 1981. She became a Sales Director in June 1982 and a National Sales Director in September 2008. Gladys says of the Mary Kay business: "Anyone who has come into Mary Kay for even one month will never be the same person. The atmosphere of friendship, honesty, and integrity leave their mark. If they learn the philosophy but don't do anything with the opportunity, they will still be a better person."
3. During the 1980s and 1990s, Mary Kay opened in these international markets: Argentina in 1980; the Dominican Republic in 1981; Uruguay in 1984; Germany in 1986; Mexico, Malaysia, and Singapore in 1986; Brunei in 1990; Guatemala, New Zealand, and Taiwan in 1991; Spain and Sweden in 1992; Russia, Norway, and the United Kingdom in 1993; China and Portugal

in 1995; the Czech Republic and Ukraine in 1997; Brazil and the Netherlands in 1998; and Hong Kong in 1999.

4. Irene Malek, "The Universality of the Golden Rule in the World Religions," *TeachingValues.com*, accessed April 11, 2020, www.teachingvalues.com/goldenrule.html.

11. MARY KAY THE CHRISTIAN

1. Mary Kay Ash, *You Can Have It All*, (Rocklin, CA: Prima Publishing, 1995), xii.
2. *You Can Have It All*, xii.
3. Mary Kay Ash, "Mary Kay Ash 700 Club Interviews," interview by Pat Robertson and Ben Kinchlow, *The 700 Club*, Christian Broadcasting Network (CBN), November 6, 1981.
4. Jill Moore began her Mary Kay business in January 1988. She became a Sales Director in 1989 and a National Sales Director in 2004. Jill is Mickey Ivey's daughter, and she says, "If I look at the people of influence in my life, the first would be my mother and then Mary Kay. I 'double dipped' because of the influence she had on my mother."
5. To learn what Mary Kay meant when she asked Kathy if she knew Jesus, see Appendix E.
6. Stacy James began her Mary Kay career in 1981. She became a Sales Director in 1983, and a National Sales Director in November 1994. She appreciates the platform Mary Kay Inc. has opened for her to speak to classrooms, church functions, and women's organizations. Stacy enjoys teaching the life lessons she has learned through Mary Kay Inc.
7. Kirk Gillespie began her Mary Kay career in July 1975. She became a Sales Director in July 1978 and a National Sales Director on August 1, 2005. When the company encouraged the sales force to collectively volunteer a million hours within their communities, she began working with her local Crisis Pregnancy Center and continues to do so today.
8. Mary Kay Inc. stopped animal testing in 1989.
9. This poem is included in Appendix D.

12. MY STORY

1. Mary Kay Ash, *You Can Have It All*, (Rocklin, CA: Prima Publishing, 1995), 169.
2. I later learned that my sister Bonita would pull these out of the trash and read them; she became a Christian at a young age.
3. For a list of books to aid in one's spiritual growth, see Appendix A.

4. Biography.com Editors, "Liberace Biography," *Biography.com*, A&E Television Networks, accessed January 29, 2020, https://www.biography.com/musician/liberace.

13. A Year of Sorrow

1. Mary Kay Ash, *Mary Kay*, (New York City: Harper & Row, Publishers, Inc., 1981), 205.
2. Spotting a purple car is such a rare occurrence that it makes me think of these verses!
3. Gelett Burgess, "The Purple Cow," *Poets.org*, 1899, https://poets.org/poem/purple-cow/.
4. Henry Wadsworth Longfellow, "A Psalm of Life," *Poets.org*, 1838, https://poets.org/poem/psalm-life.
5. Dalene White began her Mary Kay career in 1963 and debuted as one of the first two National Sales Directors in 1971. Dalene loved to talk about the times she heard Mary Kay try to explain her philosophy of Golden Rule management to businessmen. Dalene would shake her head and say, "They just couldn't get it."
6. Rena Tarbet began her Mary Kay business in June 1967. She became a Sales Director in 1970 and a National Sales Director in 1983. Diagnosed with cancer in 1973, Rena publicly lived her health battle and was an inspiration to many among the sales force and those who had been diagnosed with cancer. Rena was a dynamic speaker and writer in the fight against cancer, and her courage never faltered. She passed away in August 2013.

14. Legacy

1. Mary Kay Ash, *Mary Kay*, (Harper & Row, Publishers, Inc., 1981), 206.
2. Kristin Myers joined Mary Kay in January 2002. She became a Sales Director in November 2002 and a National Sales Director in June 2011. She feels that—other than being a nun—there is no other vocation she could have pursued that brought her closer to Jesus than her career with Mary Kay Inc.
3. Dayana Polanco joined Mary Kay Inc. in June 2008. She became a Sales Director in November 2008 and a National Sales Director in May 2011. Dayana feels that one of the biggest compliments she receives is when those who knew Mary Kay well tell her that she is just like Mary Kay.
4. Patrice Smith joined Mary Kay Inc. in June 2004. She became a Sales Director in January 2005 and a National Sales Director in December 2018. When she got her first Mary Kay datebook, filled with Mary Kay's wisdom, she would sit and read it.

5. Julia Burnett began her Mary Kay career in February 2002. She became a Sales Director in October 2002 and a National Sales Director in 2012. She is appreciative of the role Mary Kay Inc. has had in mothering her children. "My children think differently because I think differently. They have seen me set goals and miss goals; they have seen me set goals and make goals. They don't see failure as something to shy away from. Failure and success are inclusive in life."

6. Joyce Landorf Heatherly, *Balcony People*. (Salado, TX: Balcony Publishing, Inc., 1983).

7. Anonymous, "On Silver Wings," *Mary Kay World Headquarters and Museum*, (Dallas, TX: Mary Kay Cosmetics, Inc., 1995), 56.

8. Mary Kay Ash, *Mary Kay*, 3rd ed., (New York City: HarperCollins Publishers, Inc., 1994), 173, 175.

APPENDIX B

1. Mary Kay Ash, *And Stirred with Love: Recipes and Reflections Shared by the Mary Kay Family*, (Dallas, TX: Mary Kay Inc., 2002), 306.

APPENDIX C

1. Mary Kay Ash, *Cooking with Mary Kay*, (Dallas, TX: Mary Kay Inc., 1985), 198.

2. *Cooking with Mary Kay*, 196.

APPENDIX D

1. J. S. "Kirk" Kirkpatrick, "Lord, I Need To Be A Winner."

ABOUT THE AUTHOR

Photo by Barry McCoy

JENNIFER BICKEL COOK is a native Dallasite. She worked at Mary Kay Inc. while earning a bachelor's degree in English and then worked full-time after graduation. She retired from Mary Kay Inc. in 2017 after a forty-five-year association with the company, working directly with Mary Kay Ash for twenty-five of those years. Her roles at Mary Kay included manager of Mary Kay's personal staff, director of the Mary Kay Museum, and director of The Mary Kay Foundation. She lives in Irving, Texas, with her husband Rodney and her four fur persons. She has three grown children, three grandsons, and another grandchild on the way.

Mary Kay honors Anne Newbury by visiting Boston, 1972.

Mary Kay with Dorotha Dingler. Mary Kay threw the first pitch at a
St. Louis Cardinals game to raise money for cancer research, 1973.

Kirk Gillespie with Mary Kay, Mel, and fur person Gigi
at Mary Kay's round house, 1975.

Mary Kay with Sue Z. Vickers as Emily McLaughlin lovingly looks on, 1975.

Mary Kay takes time away from the Direct Selling Association Meeting in Colorado Springs to meet with Kendra Crist Cross and three of her Beauty Consultants, 1977.

Mary Kay and Jennifer's daughter, Mary Elizabeth, at the company picnic, 1979.

Jennifer and Mary Kay on Jennifer's tenth company anniversary.

The third Million Dollar Director, Wilda DeKerlegand, on a Cinderella story shopping spree with Mary Kay at Neiman Marcus, 1982.

Phyllis Pottinger with Mary Kay at her New Director Training, 1985.

Pat Danforth, Sue Kirkpatrick, and Joanne Cunnington
with Mary Kay at Southfork Ranch, 1986.

Birgit Johnson joins Mary Kay at the head table at the "Deep in the Heart" leadership conference.

Gladys Reyes (left) translating for Mary Kay at New Director Training, November 1987. Also pictured is Cecelia Garcia (right).

Mickey Ivey and her daughter, Jill
Moore Mathews, both became
National Sales Directors. Mary
Kay was always proud that the
daughters of Mary Kay leaders
wanted to follow in their
mothers' footsteps.

During the late 1980s, Mary
Kay held many events in her pink
mansion. Here she welcomes
Arlene Lenarz to her home.
Behind Arlene is Ann Sullivan.

Jennifer and her husband
Rodney at a Christmas party
for department staff and their
husbands at Mary Kay's
home, late 1980s.

Mary Kay and her staff celebrate the end of Seminar with a pool party at her home. The staff swam, and she provided the Kentucky Fried Chicken, late 1980s.

Birgit Johnson and her group from Germany in Mary Kay's office at the Addison headquarters.

Pat Danforth and her husband Tim with Mary Kay, Hawaii National Sales Director trip, 1991.

Mary Kay invites her personal staff to her home for Secretary's Day, 1991.

Mary Kay congratulates Emily McLaughlin after her speech at the National Sales Director Summit in Greenbriar, West Virginia, 1992.

Mary Kay administers the National Sales Director Oath to Sue Kirkpatrick, 1992.

Mary Kay staff member Nancy White snapped this picture backstage at Seminar before Mary Kay's memorable entrance in a horse-drawn carriage, 1993. Mary Kay expressed to Nancy that she loved horses.

Mary Kay crowns Kathy Helou as the first Sales Director whose unit reached over $2 million in sales in a year, 1993.

Ursel Elbert, the first German National Sales Director, and Mary Kay at the Dallas Seminar, 1994.

Mary Kay and Richard open awards night at Seminar 1994, the year she had her rotator cuff surgery.

Mary Kay presents Stacy James with her Million Dollar plaque at Seminar, 1995.

Jennifer boarding a helicopter with Randall Oxford (left), Mary Kay, and
Nancy Thomason (right) to fly over the Canadian Rockies, 1995.

Mary Kay and Rena Tarbet, 1996. During her thirty-eight
years of living with cancer, Rena appeared frequently with
Mary Kay to raise funds for cancer research.

Patrice Smith and her group of leaders.

Cheryl Warfield teaching at a Mary Kay Asian Future National and National Sales Director Conference in Singapore, 2009.

Julia Burnett speaking at Career Conference, 2012.

Dalene White (left) and LaQueta Collum-Fisher (right) at Dalene's last Seminar, 2014.

Dayana Polanco crowns the Queen of Sales for Mary Kay Colombia, Zorahima Cordoba, at their 2017 Seminar.

Kristin Myers with her pink Cadillac, Myers Roanoke Jumpstart, 2019.

The pink bathtub tradition continues with the new sales directors when they visit the Mary Kay Museum. Photo by Barry McCoy.

The Mary Kay Building in Addison, Texas. Photo by Barry McCoy.

Isabella Myers, daughter of Kristin Myers, visiting the Mary Kay Museum. The portrait of Mary Kay and Richard was a gift to them from the Mary Kay executive team on Mary Kay Inc.'s thirtieth anniversary.

In honor of the company's thirtieth anniversary, during Seminar,
the street leading to the convention center was renamed *Mary Kay Drive.*
Photo by Barry McCoy.